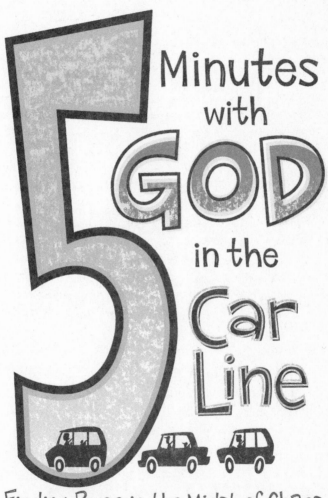

5 Minutes with God in the Car Line

Finding Pause in the Midst of Chaos

B&H
PUBLISHING GROUP

NASHVILLE, TENNESSEE

978-1-4336-4570-9

Published by B&H Publishing Group
Nashville, Tennessee

Dewey Classification: 242.643
Subject Heading: DEVOTIONAL LITERATURE
\ WOMEN \ MEDITATIONS

1 2 3 4 5 6 7 8 • 21 20 19 18 17 16

Contents

Introduction

Feed the dog. Get everyone up. Get dressed. Fix breakfast. Check the lunch money. Get out the door. Drive to the school. Go to work. Pick up the carpool. Stop by the store. Take the books back to the library. Remember, tomorrow's the day the neighbors are coming over. Start the laundry. Fix dinner. Help with geometry homework. Write a note to a friend in the hospital. Get ready for bed, so you can start it all over again. And then it hits you. The most important relationship you have, and somehow you haven't spoken to God all day.

Where in your priority list is your time with God? Finances, work concerns, family, friends—it's easy for the list to get overwhelming—but they all come second to following Christ and working to advance His kingdom.

This book gives you a chance to dive into God's Word in the short bursts of time you have throughout your day. You could do one page a day while you're waiting to pick up the kids, a few pages before bed, or any time that works for you. Some books force you into their schedule, but this one is for you. A glimpse into the Word. And then after reading, and chewing on a bit of Scripture, when you have time you can go back to the Scriptures, read the verses in their context, and allow the Holy Spirit to grow you into the Christ follower the Lord desires you to be.

Prayed for by Jesus

I have prayed for you that your faith may
not fail. And you, when you have turned
back, strengthen your brothers.
Luke 22:32

If you were to ask a passenger seated beside you on an airplane, "Do you believe in intercessory prayer?" he would possibly give you a blank stare and echo questioningly, "Intercessory?" If you explained that you meant praying on behalf of other people, they might have a grateful smile and reply, "Sure!" Most people are grateful to know that Christian friends or family members pray for them regularly.

In Luke 22:32, Christ told Peter He had prayed that Peter's faith would not fail. This prayer was effective; although Peter denied Christ, his faith led him to repent. Second, Christ requested that, after his denial and repentance, Peter would become a source of spiritual strength to his Christian friends.

The realization that Jesus, who is the same yesterday, today, and forever (Heb. 13:8), prays for all who know Him as Savior is an assuring thought (1 John 2:1). If we are grateful when our friends and family pray for us, how much more should we be thanking Jesus for speaking on our behalf? We are never standing before God alone; Christ is always standing for us.

Lord, thank You for always wanting what is best for me. Thank You for allowing me to come to You, not only on my behalf, but for others who need You to intervene in their lives. Give me the words as I pray, and help me to remember that it is not my will that I want, but Yours.

God Never Tempts

No one undergoing a trial should say, "I am being
tempted by God." For God is not tempted by
evil, and He Himself doesn't tempt anyone.
James 1:13

Professionals who deal with offenders in our criminal justice system often note how seldom convicts admit to personal guilt. Many tend to regard their crimes as the fault of someone else. This is not just a habit within prison; look at children when they get caught doing something they know they are not supposed to be doing. Our first instinct is to blame someone else. That kind of thinking is unbiblical in regard to human sin. This passage in James prohibits blaming God for our temptations. It needs no interpretation, just acceptance. Sometimes, we foster our own temptations by putting ourselves into dishonorable situations that reflect unwholesome personal desires. At times, we may try to credit God with every wrong turn we take in life, saying, "He made me like this!" Believers must accept personal responsibility for wrong actions. When we become willing to put the blame for sin on the right shoulders—our own—and ask for forgiveness, then, "He is faithful and righteous to forgive us our sins and to cleanse us from all unrighteousness" (1 John 1:9)

Lord, please help me today to take responsibility for my own actions. Help me to remember that even when circumstances are not my doing, my reaction to them are always my responsibility. I know that I am going to mess up, and thank You for forgiving me and pulling me back up when I fall down.

Be Serious and Alert

Be serious! Be alert! Your adversary the
Devil is prowling around like a roaring lion,
looking for anyone he can devour.
1 Peter 5:8

Your day is scheduled down to the minute, plus you have the extra list of things that you can check off if you get a chance. At home you have a TV, in the car you have a radio, walking you have your phone. Do you ever get the feeling you are being pulled in a million different directions? In a world filled with distractions, a Christian needs to maintain both a clear mind and a keen vision when dealing with the devil.

In this Scripture, Satan is characterized as a hungry lion stalking a flock of sheep: prowling, ready to pounce and to destroy the lambs. No doubt Peter, the inspired author of these verses, recalled the aching memory of his denial of his Savior, a time when he became afraid to stand for Christ and surrendered to temptation. When alone in a field the lamb may notice the distant lion, but we are not in an empty field. We are in a hall of mirrors, complete with lights, music, and moving parts. There are hiding places everywhere. The Christian must evidence a sane mind and a posture of readiness. We must know the traps we fall into, and the distractions that lead us into the lion's mouth.

Lord, help me to be watchful, and always on alert. Help me to not be distracted by the things of this world, but to keep my eye on you. Make my temptations so clear that I have no problem avoiding them. Be with me when I fall prey to the lion, and pull me back again.

Submit to God

Therefore, submit to God. But resist
the Devil, and he will flee from you.
James 4:7

Many years ago a Methodist preacher stood on the streets of London's East End and saw hundreds of people trapped in poverty, filth, and vice. Here he discovered an arena in which a Christian could work, but few were willing to try. He later wrote that God spoke to him and told him that would be his field of service. Arriving home late one evening after having preached in a tent revival, he told his wife he had committed their lives to serve in the East End of London. They knelt together, prayed, and accepted God's assignment.

This was the scary part of town. The part of town that you do not go to alone—even in daylight. The part of town that you definitely do not let your children go to; and yet because this preacher heard from God, his whole family was now submitting to service.

The man was William Booth, and the work he began is now known worldwide as the Salvation Army. Booth heard God's call and submitted his life to Him without reservation. As a result, millions have met the Savior and been delivered from sin and Satan's grasp. God does not always ask us to do what is easy, safe, or even what the world considers smart. He pulls His children to places where only He can see the path. It is here that we can have complete faith. When lives are submitted to the control and guidance of the Holy Spirit, they are unconquerable.

Father, make me submissive so I may be usable. Help me to remember that my trust is not in the safety I have created for myself, but in Your ultimate power in all situations. Open my ears to be able to hear Your voice when you call me, and give me the strength to follow that call, no matter where it leads.

Don't Follow the Crowd

My son, if sinners entice you,
don't be persuaded.
Proverbs 1:10

"If a man does not keep pace with his companions," wrote Henry David Thoreau, "perhaps it is because he hears a different drummer. Let him step to the music which he hears, however measured or far away."[1] The writer of Proverbs likewise advised a young man to refuse to follow the crowd and conform to the way of sin.

Today, as always, the temptation is to follow the crowd. All of us live under constant pressure to conform, to pattern our lives to fit the designs of others. Be on the latest diet, wear the coolest clothes, parent the way society tells you, be more disciplined in your workout than your prayer time, make sure you're up-to-date on pop culture, and do not forget to sell the most cookies for the fund raiser. We are constantly fighting to stay in step with the music of the world, when God has given us a different beat to follow. The temptation is not the problem. Even the Son of God was tempted by Satan to take the easy, popular way. The problem comes when we give in or try to mix the two beats together. God does not remove us from temptation any more than He did His Son. However, God's people do not have to be helpless victims of temptation. We are responsible for the way we behave when temptation arrives, for keeping on following the "music" of the Lord's voice. Focus on God's beat and you'll never fall out of step.

Father, help me to let You direct my walk. Make it clear to me where in my life I'm following You, and where I have allowed the world to take over. Make Your music so loud that I cannot even hear the beat other people are following.

---

1. Walden, *Life in the Woods*, 1854.

Watch and Pray

Stay awake and pray so that you won't enter into
temptation. The spirit is willing, but the flesh is weak.
Mark 14:38

If the person to whom you had anchored your life and pledged unfailing allegiance was betrayed by a traitor, manhandled by a mob, ordered beaten by a cowardly governor, and crucified by soldiers from a nearby Roman garrison, would you become afraid? Absolutely! The temptation facing Jesus' disciples during the days surrounding Jesus' death was nothing less than to panic and to run. The Son of God recognized this in advance; before His arrest, during His personal agony in the garden, He shared with His disciples the way to react to every kind of temptation.

While we all have not found ourselves in this exact situation, we all have at one point been overwhelmed and ready to run. Jesus told the disciples to watch and to pray, and His method is just as relevant to us now. When you are scared of the unknown—watch and pray. When you feel overwhelmed by temptation—watch and pray. When you do not know anything else to do—watch and pray.

Help me, Lord, to watch and to pray. Give me the words to pray, and the wisdom to know that even when I don't know the words, You do. Keep my eyes open to see You working in my life, and to see when You give me opportunities to move. Grant me patience, and help me to remember that Your timing is perfect and far better than my own.

From Dead to Alive

But God, who is rich in mercy, because of His
great love that He had for us, made us alive
with the Messiah even though we were dead
in trespasses. You are saved by grace!
Ephesians 2:4-5

Have you ever placed a dull brown bulb in the earth and seen in the spring a fresh, beautiful lily breaking through the ground in its place? Or do you remember how delighted you were the first time you saw that the little caterpillar, so neatly wrapped, had burst forth transformed into a lovely, colorful butterfly?

There is an even greater and more beautiful change in a person when God brings them to life through Christ. The ordinance of baptism is symbolic of dying to our old life and rising to walk in a new way of life (Rom. 6:4). Baptism testifies to others of the miraculous change in a new believer's life; but it is not what makes the change in the person. It is God's grace that brings us to life when we are dead.

Thank You for seeing me when I was still lost in my sin and for pouring out Your grace on me so that I could be alive! Help me to live so that others can see Your power. Remind me every day that this life is a gift from You, and help me to live it according to Your will, and not following into the habits that I had while I was still dead. Thank You, Father, for my new life in You.

The Broken Wall

For He is our peace, who made both groups one
and tore down the dividing wall of hostility.
Ephesians 2:14

After World War II, the city of Berlin, Germany, was divided into sections, resulting in a wall between East and West Berlin. There came to be a great difference in life on the two sides of this wall. While those on the west side were free, those on the east side were quite limited. Trying to escape from East Berlin meant certain death. The news that this wall had finally been broken down brought joy around the world. It showed the end of the war, and redemption of a city.

In the temple, there was a curtain that separated the Holy of Holies. Only the high priest was allowed to go through and sacrifice to God. The Scriptures record the tearing of this veil when Jesus died on the cross (Matt. 27:51). This is cause for celebration! This event demonstrated that through Christ's redemptive sacrifice, God has allowed believers direct access to Himself.

As Ephesians 2:14 records, this curtain was not the only wall that Jesus brought down with His sacrifice. There had been a spiritual wall between Jews and everyone else. The Jews were God's chosen people and no one else could have access to Him. With Jesus' resurrection, He made salvation available to all people!

Thank You, Lord, for offering me access to You and spiritual kinship with all believers in Christ. Thank You for bringing all Your children together as one people, and for always being available to us, no matter where we are.

Empowered to Serve

I was made a servant of this gospel by
the gift of God's grace that was given
to me by the working of His power.
Ephesians 3:7

When asked to serve on a committee or in a ministry of our churches, many of us, perhaps, have felt like responding, "I can't accept this position because I am not capable," or "I'm sorry I don't have time," or maybe even, "that's not what I want to do." God does gift different persons with different abilities, and just because someone asks you to do something does not mean that God is calling you to say yes, but if God is calling you to serve He will give you the ability, time, and eventually desire you need to do so. We are never capable of serving in our own strength. When we try, we always fail. It is only when we depend on God's power that we accomplish His will in serving.

In this Scripture, Paul described the power of God that made him a minister. Every Christian is called by God to serve in some way, and when God calls a person to serve, He always provides that person with the power to serve effectively. "God's grace" has been defined as "unmerited favor." Paul's words remind us that when we give our time and talents to God, it is God that gives us time and talents and lets us use them to serve Him.

God, empower me in Your service. Help me to remember that it's not about me, it's just about You. Help me to see the opportunities that You have placed before me. Guide me when to say yes, even if it is outside my comfort zone.

A Timely Caravan

When Midianite traders passed by, his brothers pulled
Joseph out of the pit and sold him for 20 pieces of
silver to the Ishmaelites, who took Joseph to Egypt.
Genesis 37:28

Jealousy is ugly, whether between spouses, friends, or siblings.
Parents can unwittingly contribute to sibling rivalry by showing
favoritism to one child over another. Have you ever been able to just
tell that someone was the favorite, even if it was never directly said?
Jacob made it pretty clear that Joseph was his favorite by giving him
a special garment, which was the final spark to ignite the jealousy
of Jacob's other sons toward their younger brother. Of course,
Joseph didn't exactly help the situation by sharing his dreams of
his brothers bowing down to him. Their hatred increased, and they
made plans to dispose of their little brother. At first they planned
to kill him, but later they saw an opportunity to make a profit by
selling him into slavery. They never expected to see Joseph again.
God had other plans. God used the caravan that came by to spare
Joseph from a deadly fate and to move him along in God's ultimate
plan. Eventually, the Lord would use Joseph to save the lives of
Jacob and all his sons.

We think we know when something bad is happening, or when
something good is happening, but the truth is we have no idea the
grand plan that God has in mind. All we can do is trust that God
has the big picture, and that what others intend for evil, He will use
for good.

*Dear Lord, may I ever be mindful that You can use all things for Your
purpose and glory. Help me to see my circumstances with Your eyes rather
than my own.*

Restored

But when they told Jacob all that Joseph had
said to them, and when he saw the wagons
that Joseph had sent to transport him, the
spirit of their father Jacob revived.
Genesis 45:27

Two brothers had not spoken for thirty years. One became ill and decided to go to his brother to make peace. He was gladly received. The amazing thing was neither could recall why they had quit speaking! Have you ever held onto a feud or grudge that you did not even remember who started? The forgiveness between these brothers is similar to the reconciliation experienced by Joseph and his brothers. Joseph had every reason to hold onto bitterness from what his brothers had done. Despite everything that had happened, Joseph considered himself blessed. Eventually, Joseph assumed a position in the pharaoh's court that made him responsible for administering the nation's crop storage and distribution system. This led to his being reunited with his family. His father had grieved over his loss. He had grieved over the broken relationships in his family. He was broken. Upon learning that Joseph had sent for him, Jacob's zest for life was restored beyond anything he likely ever expected to feel again. Reconciliation is always difficult—and it is the first step that is the hardest. If you have a relationship in your life that needs to be restored, do all you can to take the initiative and make it happen.

Dear Lord, help me to be a peacemaker where there is estrangement. Help me to seek forgiveness for the wrongs I have committed against others and to forgive others—regardless of their desire for such forgiveness. Give me opportunities to be the catalyst for change.

Want Something Priceless?

Happy is a man who finds wisdom and
who acquires understanding.
Proverbs 3:13

When God offered him the desire of his heart, Solomon, the son of David, requested wisdom. In this passage Solomon offered explanation of the value of wisdom. Wisdom is more valuable than the most known riches of gold, silver, and rubies. Wisdom must be searched for, but when found and gained, wisdom is pleasant and offers a path of peace. Through wisdom, we gain ultimate understanding and can start to see some of the plan of God's will.

We often pray for the outcome we want, but have you ever prayed for wisdom and discernment? Have you ever, when faced with a difficult situation, prayed that you would know what to do, and how to respond, whether the result went your way or not? We are wandering around in the dark asking God to remove our obstacles, but we haven't asked Him to turn on the light. Wisdom is not something we have naturally, or that we acquire over time. Knowledge comes from experience—wisdom comes from God.

Father, thank You for Your guidance and the offer of wisdom. Lord, turn on the light and help me to see and understand Your plan. Give me discernment for what is Your will and what is not. Help me to learn as You teach so that I will be ready to offer wisdom to another.

People of Integrity

But let your word "yes" be "yes," and your "no" be
"no." Anything more than this is from the evil one.
Matthew 5:37

On a hillside with a crowd, Jesus called them all to sit down, and He began to teach. Jesus spoke with both authority and tenderness, offering clarity to what they had heard before. So many rules His listeners had been instructed to follow. At this point in His teaching, Jesus simply reminded them—tell the truth, be a person of honor. No need for further amplification, just the truth. If people know you as someone with integrity, will they need any more than yes or no?

When someone asks for a promise or an oath, what they are really saying is, "I believe . . . almost." They want you to recognize that it is testing their trust to believe you. They want you to feel the weight of your answer—and they may be doing this without even realizing it. How often do you ask someone that you claim to trust if they are "sure"? Jesus tells us in Matthew that one *yes* should be enough. We should be trusted so much that no one even needs to ask us a second time, because they know our first answer is final, and what we say we will follow through with.

Father, help me to be faithful with my "yes" or "no" so that others know I can be fully trusted. Help me to realize when I am breaking someone's trust, and give me ways to beg forgiveness and redeem my word in their eyes. Help me to be faithful to what I say and earn the trust of those around me.

Discerning Favor

Good will come to a man who lends generously
and conducts his business fairly.
Psalm 112:5

God has a deep, genuine concern about the way we look at and handle the provisions in our lives. After all, we know He is a good Father who watches out for His children. When a psalm begins with "Praise the Lord" or "Hallelujah," it's an automatic reminder that any review of God's provisions for us should begin with adoration and exaltation. As we see what God has given—whether it is little or much—we recognize that it comes from His hand. We are blessed spiritually and, at times, blessed with material gifts as well. For our spiritual growth, we must decide how to handle the favor of God in our lives.

This passage tells us that "good" will come to those who are generous and honest; but what does "good" mean? We must learn to discern that God's favor is not just material, but spiritual. His spiritual blessings are certainly more significant. Additionally, the spiritual blessings help us to know how to use the material ones. With a generous life, we draw closer to Christ and are conformed to His image.

Father, thank You for blessing me so that I may be a blessing to others. Help me today to remember that not all of Your blessings are material, and whatever I have You have called me to share with others. Give me opportunities to be generous.

Want a Clear Conscience?

I always do my best to have a clear
conscience toward God and men.
Acts 24:16

As we go about working in the mission of God, our character often will be called into question. Our motives will be scrutinized, and our actions will be judged. In the early church, Paul often defended himself before the accusations of many people, including those who were politically powerful and those who were the religious leaders of the day. We will likely not be called upon to answer for our faith in court, but we must be able to give a witness for our faith in the culture. It begins with living in such a way that God is pleased with our lives. Our integrity before others is dependent upon our integrity before God. As we daily submit to the work of Christ in our lives, then our character is changed to mirror that of Jesus. Paul described the experience of having a clear conscience so that others would know he was certain of what he believed. Our actions will always show off our true beliefs. If we want to have a conscience like Paul, we must have similar convictions—and hold to them. The only way to a clear conscience? Have a sure faith.

Father, empower me by the work of Your Holy Spirit so that I may live out my faith. I know it is only through Your power that I can live honestly. Help me be sure in my faith and in my steps. When I fall, as I know I will, give me the courage to be open and honest about my faults and not try to hide them. Give me Your strength.

True Success

Sitting down, He called the Twelve and said
to them, "If anyone wants to be first, he
must be last of all and servant of all."
Mark 9:35

Success is a common topic of discussion in our lives. In raising
children, we teach them about the true meaning of success.
Wherever we work, we want to be successful. In our leisure time and
hobbies, we want the accomplishment of winning a game, finishing
a hike, or completing yard work. At the end of it all, we know that
success is more than completing work for self-satisfaction. It is more
than making the most money or having the biggest office. This is
a lesson even the Twelve apostles struggled through. They actually
argued about who was the most successful among their group in
the eyes of Jesus. Knowing their argument, Jesus gave them an
unexpected and shocking answer. The impact of His response has
not lost any of its power when we read it today. In God's economy,
success comes in using power on behalf of others. Jesus' illustration
of serving a child was scandalous to first-century men. But He
wanted to show that true success comes through serving others. Just
as Jesus used His power to serve us through going to the cross, we
must use the strength He gives us to serve others.

*Father, put in me a heart for serving others. Help me to judge myself not
by the standards of the world, but by Your standards alone. Make serving
others be my desire, and remove my selfish ambition.*

Boldness and Access

In Him we have boldness and confident
access through faith in Him.
Ephesians 3:12

In ancient times, a king's subjects often came trembling before him. They bowed in humility, fearing to present their requests.

In the book of Esther, we can see the story of Queen Esther (Hadassah) who hesitated to go unbidden into King Ahasuerus's presence, even though he was her husband. The penalty for approaching the king unbidden was death, unless he accepted the petitioner's presence by extending his scepter. Esther's people, the Jews, had been threatened with extinction. Mordecai, her cousin, challenged her to be brave and to approach the king to speak on behalf of the Jews (Esther 4:8, 14).

The God we worship is much greater and more powerful than any earthly king. Though we should come before Him in humility, we need not fear or hesitate. He made us, He loves us, and He is accessible at all times. We can come boldly with confidence that He cares and will answer our prayers. This privilege of access was given to us by Christ's death on the cross. We can go directly to God through Jesus our Savior, in whom we put our faith.

Thank You, Lord, for Jesus, who made our access to You possible and gives us confidence to approach You. Thank You for being all powerful and always accepting me when I approach You.

More Than We Ask

Now to Him who is able to do above and
beyond all that we ask or think according
to the power that works in us.
Ephesians 3:20

When you make a request of someone, isn't it pleasant to have him or her do more than you ask? We all enjoy that extra, unexpected act from others, but it is never our first instinct.

God always gives us more that we deserve, and even more than we ask for. God's spiritual blessings are more than generous. Ephesians 3:15–19 lists magnificent, life transforming examples: inward strength from God's Spirit; the indwelling of Christ by faith; a deep comprehension of the dimensions of God's love; a life fulfilled "with all the fullness of God." These are some of the spiritual riches God wants to give Christians, and these are "above and beyond all that we ask or think" (Eph. 3:20).

We cannot out-give God. However much or little we do for Him, it does not affect the outpouring that He gives us. Someone once said, "The most I can do for God is the least I can afford to do." He always gives more than we ask.

Thank You, Lord, for Your abundant blessings. Thank You for knowing what I need better than I know myself. Thank You for giving me so much more than I could dream to ask for. Help me to remember that Your plans are greater than my plans and to trust in Your ultimate plan.

Power to Build Up

From Him the whole body, fitted and knit together
by every supporting ligament, promotes the
growth of the body for building up itself in love
by the proper working of each individual part.
Ephesians 4:16

Paul used the analogy of the body to refer to those who have been redeemed by Christ and who are working together in God's kingdom. Christ is the head, of course. Then we (Christians) are the various parts "fitly joined together" to form the body. If we are each performing our proper function, the body will work together effectively.

This body is not to be a mere machine. It is not to operate in a routine, lifeless manner. While each part has a different job, every member has the job to lift up the others in the body. The power that edifies (builds up) comes from Christ and demonstrates itself in love between God's children. Love comes from God: "God is love" (1 John 4:8). Thus, Christ, the head of the body, and the source of love, imparts that love to each of us who open our hearts to Him and enter His kingdom. In love and unity, the body can grow and develop, as it should, as Christ's redeeming work is continued.

God, help me examine my life to see if I am allowing Your power through me to edify the "body of Christ." Help me to love well; the way that You do. Keep me strong as a member of the body of Christ and show me opportunities to support others in the body.

Power of Truth

Since you put away lying, Speak the truth,
each one to his neighbor, because we
are members of one another.
Ephesians 4:25

What if you couldn't trust your eyes and your brain to tell your feet the truth? You'd fall down all the time. Your mobility would be seriously threatened because your whole body couldn't function effectively as a unit.

Everyone appreciates honesty. Telling the truth makes us more able to work together. We know this; nevertheless, we often fail to recognize that when we break faith with other people we damage ourselves. This is especially true in the church. We are Christ's body, and the function of the body as a whole is dependent on the effective working together of the parts.

Lying is not an acceptable practice for Christians. Paul admonished Christians to put off the behavior of the "old man" (who we were before being saved) and to "put on the new man." This is like a beggar discarding his rags and putting on princely robes. Then Christ's body will be able to work together effectively and will look much more attractive to those yet unsaved.

Lord, give me power to be honest in word and deed. Help me remember the importance of keeping my word and supporting the body of Christ.

Moments to Remember

Then Joshua set up in Gilgal the 12 stones
they had taken from the Jordan.
Joshua 4:20

Memories are powerful. Thoughts of times we spent with a family member, experiences we had as children, special trips with the family, or times of overcoming adversity provide encouragement and hope. These memories are the blocks upon which current days are built. We have lots of different ways to remind of the good times. You may have pictures in a scrapbook or a ticket stub in a drawer, maybe even some dried flowers hanging on the wall. The children of Israel had experienced God's deliverance from slavery and the exodus. Now they were on the cusp of receiving the promised land that would sustain the future of their people. But God did not want them to forget how it had happened. To forget was to dismiss. In the Israelites' future, forgetting proved to be tragic each time they forgot the Lord's goodness to them. The same is true in our lives. We have so many blessings to remember: the spiritual strength God gives to fight temptation, the grace to forgive when we are wronged, and more. But foremost we should remember the moment that Christ forgave us of sin and gave us eternal life. We may not need to put twelve boulders in a pile in our yard, but we should remember daily the good work of God in our lives.

Father, thank You for Your gracious work to save my soul and strengthen me each day. Give me daily reminders of Your grace in my life. Help me use the past and not forget what You have done for me.

Quiet Giving

But when you give to the poor, don't let your
left hand know what your right hand is doing.
Matthew 6:3

One of the most difficult things in life is to be unnoticed. We are not always looking for a parade in our honor but a proverbial "pat on the back" never hurts. Right? Wrong. As Jesus taught on the life of faith, He reminded us that giving must be done simply for the sake of giving. When done for show, approval, or applause, it ruins the purpose. Rather than focusing on the one in need, we ask everyone to focus on us. This passage in Matthew's Gospel is clear. We should be givers. In fact, the Heavenly Father wants to reward us for doing so. Just as He looks after the poor and the outcast, so should His people. In this sermon from Jesus, He gives us the necessary guidance about how to do well at giving. The key Jesus points to is to give quietly, perhaps, even anonymously. As we mature in our faith, this kind of giving allows us to not be the center of attention. Now does that mean the giving does not mean as much if anyone finds out about it? Of course not, but by keeping it to yourself, you guard yourself from the temptation of wanting praise. By growing up, we will place others before the Lord for their needs to be met. As He makes use of us in the work, we find our full reward in our relationship with Him.

Father, please form my heart to be like Yours. Give me opportunities to be generous toward others. Cleanse my heart of the desire for praise. Remind me daily to give for the one that is in need and not for my own reasons.

24

Light in the Dark

It came between the Egyptian and Israelite forces. The
cloud was there in the darkness, yet it lit up the night.
So neither group came near the other all night long.
Exodus 14:20

Pharaoh had second thoughts about having released the Hebrews, and he pursued them. Israel's situation appeared hopeless, except for God. Lying in front of Israel was the Red Sea. Behind them was the Egyptian army. Miraculously, the angel of God and a pillar of cloud went behind Israel, separating them from the Egyptians so that neither came near the other all night. God was in the cloud to envelop the Egyptians in darkness while giving light to Israel. God then parted the waters, allowing Israel to go through on dry land. Pharaoh's hosts drowned.

Have you ever been in a situation that seemed hopeless? Have you ever felt trapped, with darkness all around? God is light. He always lights the way for His people through the darkness. His Word is a light to life's path (Ps. 119:105). Moreover, Jesus came saying, "I am the light of the world" (John 8:12). Making our way through the world's darkness requires being in a faith relationship with Jesus and abiding in His Word daily. If you have God with you, you are never trapped or hopeless. He will always be there to guide your steps, and give you a way out.

Lord, help me to remember that I am never alone. You are light; enlighten my way through today's darkness. Do not let me become lost or trapped by the things of this world.

Misplaced Confidence

Woe to those who go down to Egypt for help
and who depend on horses! They trust in the
abundance of chariots and in the large number
of horsemen. They do not look to the Holy One
of Israel and they do not seek the LORD's help.

Isaiah 31:1

Historians might point out, quite rightly, that it would have been safer for Judah to have been thrown in with Assyria rather than gambling on Egypt's help. But the problem was not that Judah chose the wrong ally; its fatal mistake was that Judah failed to choose God.

Finding a replacement to rely on is a common temptation. Perhaps, our Egypt is technology. We are awed by it, depend upon it, and revel in it. How wonderful it is to communicate with loved ones on the other side of the world via the Internet. How fun it is to be in community enjoying a good movie. How convenient it is, even in a foreign country, to be able to use a debit card to get currency from a personal bank account. And what remarkable miracles are performed by medical science! There's nothing wrong with benefitting from technological marvels so long as we regard them as gifts from God rather than replacements for God. We must never forget that God alone is our salvation!

Lord, in this age of amazing human accomplishment, keep my faith grounded in Your providential care. Help me to remember who is my true provider, and where all of these supplies come from. Keep me humble!

Strength Is Not Enough

A king is not saved by a large army; a warrior
will not be delivered by great strength.
Psalm 33:16

The Maginot Line was the most elaborate fortification system Europe had ever seen. This bastion of steel and concrete, costing half a billion dollars, stretched along the eastern border of France. It consisted of a series of huge underground forts on six levels, barracks of 3,000,000 troops, ammunition dumps, power stations for ventilation and lighting, miniature railroads, kitchens, hospitals, and ground-level guns nestled in heavy casements and served by ammunition hoists—all of it invulnerable to shells and bombs. This was a so-called impregnable fortress, but that didn't stop Hitler's regiments. They simply went around it in their drive towards Paris.

Other names, such as *Titanic*, remind us that in the realm of human endeavor, there are no guarantees. No matter how strong something seems, there is always an iceberg that can take it down. Is there anything in life that can be counted on? Yes! We sing about it. "On Christ the solid Rock I stand; all other ground is sinking sand." Christ alone can stand up against anything and always come out victorious. He alone is the strength that will always be enough.

Lord, help me not to misplace my hopes. I know I get distracted by the strength of this world, but help me to remember that Your strength is my only true salvation. Remind me daily to rely only on You!

Arrogant Pride

The king exclaimed, "Is this not Babylon the Great
that I have built by my vast power to be a royal
residence and to display my majestic glory?"
Daniel 4:30

If every sports fan who wags an index finger in the air proclaiming,
"We're number one!" is telling the truth, we have at least a thousand
number-one teams every football season. This self-proclaiming
tendency is nothing new to humanity. The monarchs of Assyria
assumed the title "King of Universal Reign." The haughtiness of
Nebuchadnezzar knew no geographical bounds. In his inaugural
address, he prayed to the pagan god Marduk that he might receive
"tribute of the kinds of all regions, from all mankind." Centuries
later, the Roman Emperor Domitian insisted on being addressed as
"Our Lord and God."

It doesn't matter now what these rulers thought of themselves,
because no matter what they said or what they demanded, they
were proved wrong. They died a human death, just like everyone
else. The only one who deserves to have such pride, is the most
humble person to have ever lived—Jesus Christ. And He proved
His greatness above all the false rulers when He rose again from the
dead. True wisdom is shown by someone like John the Baptist, who
said of Jesus, "He must increase, but I must decrease" (John 3:30).
John, in his humility and faith, earned a number-one spot (Matt.
11:11) in Jesus' estimation.

*Lord, grant me a healthy confidence that is not rooted in self-serving
arrogance. Help me to make more of You and less of me.*

The Purpose of Scripture

All Scripture is inspired by God and is
profitable for teaching, for rebuking, for
correcting, for training in righteousness,
2 Timothy 3:16

When a person knows his words are his last, they often want to make sure they are the most important. In this last letter to his disciple Timothy, Paul was adamant about the purpose and value of God's Word. Paul never wasted time or influence. Obviously he valued the Scriptures highly (2 Tim. 4:13).

The Bible was written by men who were divinely inspired by God. By His Spirit, God breathed His holy breath upon the human authors who penned the precise words He desired. He did not override their personalities or wills but worked through them to produce the Word from God that is without error; thus, it is totally true and trustworthy. Christians who study the Bible and apply what they learn will grow in holiness and avoid many pitfalls in this world. All of Scripture points to the gospel. The Old Testament Scriptures point to Christ, revealing the depth of our sin and our need for a Savior. The Gospels reveal Christ as that Savior, and the remaining New Testament instructs us how to live out our faith in Him.

Father, thank You for a clear revelation of truth and for detailed instructions on how to live in this world for Your glory. Help me as I read Scripture to remember that the entirety of Scripture is correct, and without error, and help me to interpret the words in truth.

Instructions Needed

He began to speak boldly in the synagogue. After
Priscilla and Aquila heard him, they took him home and
explained the way of God to him more accurately.
Acts 18:26

Some people are prone to shoot first and aim later. When we assemble something purchased at the department store, we only read the instructions when we get stuck (usually because we didn't read the instructions first). We get lost before asking for directions. We jump and hope there is something to catch us. Apollos was a "get it done" person. The Scripture attributes many good qualities to him (eloquent, mighty, fervent, accurate), but all the good human qualities in the world don't make a person right, especially if he doesn't have all the facts. That's where the apostle Paul and his fellow church planters found Apollos—with half the story. Two important things happened next: The disciples confronted Apollos humbly with the truth, and he received it humbly. Obviously, the Holy Spirit was at work! Can you picture today a church leader telling another church leader that they were giving the wrong message? We have these confrontations constantly, but how often are they given and received in humility. We all need instructions in daily living. We all have times that we did not get the whole story right. We must constantly seek truth in God's Word. Are you reading the instruction manual?

Lord, grant me the humility to help others and to receive help when I need it. Remind me that no matter how well I know Your Word, I should never be so arrogant to think I know it all perfectly. I am fallible; it is only Your Word that is perfect.

Surface Appeal

No man in all Israel was as handsome and highly
praised as Absalom. From the sole of his foot to
the top of his head, he did not have a single flaw.
2 Samuel 14:25

Who has not heard the phrase, "Beauty is only skin deep"? This is only a partially true statement. There are many people who are beautiful inside and out. The real meaning of the phrase cautions against judging solely on the basis of outward appearance. David must have taken great pride in his beloved son Absalom. The root word in Absalom's name means peace. Absalom was a baby any dad would rejoice over, big and strong with a tremendous head of thick, curly hair. While no man was as highly praised for his outward appearance, Absalom's beauty was only skin deep. Absalom turned out to be a murderer and an insurrectionist who brought great heartache to his family. This baby, who once brought great peace, became a man who turned King David's world upside down.

Our culture today encourages us to focus on outward beauty while constantly tempting the inner decay of our morals and character. God looks on the inside, not at the surface. He desires us to focus on the states of our hearts.

Lord, teach me to prefer a pure heart for You rather than outward beauty and the approval of people. Help me to see others as You see them. Remind me to look at a person's character rather than their outward appearance.

He Became Sin for Us

He made the One who did not know sin to
be sin for us, so that we might become
the righteousness of God in Him.
2 Corinthians 5:21

You've probably made an exchange at a clothing store at some point in your life. Suppose you receive a new sweater for your birthday, but it does not fit you properly. What will you do? You will probably take it back to the clothing store and exchange it for a sweater that fits better. The picture of an exchange comes to mind when we think about what Christ has done for us. As humans, sin fits us all too well. Each of us has sinned against God, and we deserve the penalty that goes along with being sinners. Being righteous fits Jesus to a tee—He "did not know sin" (v. 21). He never sinned, and He has always been right with God. At Calvary, Jesus made the greatest exchange ever known. He became sin for us so that we could become right with God. Because of that extravagant exchange at Calvary, we can enjoy eternal life as God's children and look forward to our home in heaven. Because of Christ, that relationship fits us best of all.

Father, thank You for sending Your Son Jesus, who never sinned, to become sin for me so I could be right with You. I deserve death for my sins, but Jesus took on this punishment and in exchange gave me eternal life! Help me to never forget this ultimate sacrifice.

God's Restoration

After Job had prayed for his friends,
the LORD restored his prosperity and
doubled his previous possessions.
Job 42:10

The miserable ordeal that consumed Job's life had finally come to an end. He had lost everything he treasured, including his health. Throughout the ordeal, he wondered if the Lord had deserted him. But a new day had dawned for him, thanks to the Lord's work of restoration. The Lord restored Job's life as he began to pray for his friends, even though they actually had not been good or helpful to him at all. They insisted that his agony was his own fault and that God was punishing him. Of course, what they told Job turned out to be wrong. But instead of resenting them for what they had said, he prayed for them. Instead of being self-centered, he turned his heart toward his misguided friends. Job's story reminds us that the Lord can restore what's been lost.

Relationships are hard. They take work. There is no relationship that does not take sacrifice and compromise on both sides. When a relationship breaks, it is only with God's power that it can be truly restored. But when He provides restoration, He will do it in His time and in His way. What can we do? We can read God's Word and pray. Instead of praying only for ourselves, we do well to pray for others who need to be restored.

Father, turn my troubled heart to others and to the full assurance that I can count on You. Help me to give forgiveness to those who have steered me wrong, and guide my prayers to be others focused.

Spirit vs. Flesh

I say then, walk by the Spirit and you will
not carry out the desire of the flesh.
Galatians 5:16

Children of all ages like to play tug-of-war. As they team up on
either end of a long rope, they combine their strength so they can
pull the opposing team across the center line. The struggle shows
itself in the tension placed on the rope. A tough competition like
tug-of-war provides a great image of the stress we may face as we
seek to serve the Lord. Our struggles in discipleship are revealed
in the tension pulling us in two directions at the same time. The
tug-of-war puts a strain on our walk with Him. Paul wrote about
the tension in terms of the Spirit and the flesh. Because we belong
to Christ, we want to follow the leadership of the Holy Spirit in a
selfless way. But we have to resist the temptation to feed the sinful,
selfish indulgences—"the lust of the flesh"—that do not honor the
Lord. Paul teaches us that winning the battle every day starts by
walking in the Spirit. Each day finds us prayerfully resolving that
we are going to follow and obey Jesus step by step.

*Father, show me the steps You want me to take today so I can walk in Your
Spirit as I seek to fulfill Your purposes for my life. Make the desires of my
flesh weak and the strength of my spirit strong, so that I am able to follow
You with full confidence.*

Divinely Induced Fear

Each Israelite took his position around
the camp, and the entire Midianite army
fled, and cried out as they ran.
Judges 7:21

Sometimes fear can be helpful. It can alert a person to danger, and God can use it to stop His enemies in their tracks. God gave Gideon a plan for defeating the Midianites who had been troubling Israel. The plan involved fear—on both sides. Gideon ordered his small army of three hundred Israelites to surround the mighty Midianites as they camped in the valley. They knew they were outnumbered. He instructed each man to take a trumpet, an empty jar, and a torch and then stand on the surrounding hillside to wait for his command. In the middle of the night, Gideon ordered his men to blow their trumpets, smash their jars, and hold up their torches. They were spread thin and loudly announcing their presence. They were brave and followed the plan that God had laid out. The scene they created struck fear in the Midianite camp. Thinking that they had been surrounded by a superior fighting machine, the unsuspecting Midianite soldiers scattered in horror. God's plan worked! He used fear to protect His people. God's plans always work. He knows what He wants to accomplish in and through us. He knows the results. We can trust Him to protect and care for His people.

Father, thank You for always doing what is in the best interest of Your people. Thank You for being worthy of all my trust. You are the only one deserving my obedience.

Do You Believe?

Then Jesus said to him, "'If You can?' Everything
is possible to the one who believes."
Mark 9:23

The little word *if* is simple to spell. Even though it's a tiny word, it can create a huge problem for us when we use it to avoid trusting the Lord. The worried father of a troubled child discovered that using "if" complicated his conversation with Jesus. He had brought his child to Jesus' disciples, but they couldn't do anything to help. That's when Jesus showed up and began to talk to him about his child's problem. In the conversation, he implored Jesus to do something *if* He could. Jesus responded to the frustrated father by calling his "if" into question. The Lord could handle anything. Therefore, no word that implied doubt belonged in the conversation. Only the word *believe* would suit the situation. Jesus encouraged him to replace doubt with faith in Him. Doubt makes us use *if* when we're seeking the Lord's help. Faith compels us to replace it with *believe*. By trusting the Lord, we can live in the full assurance that nothing we bring to Him will be too tough for Him to handle. Is anything too hard for God?

Father, because I believe in You, I will erase the "if" from my conversation with You. I will remember that You have full power in all situations. Lord, strengthen my faith, and help me to be obedient to You in all situations.

Time to Stop Crying

This is what the LORD says: "Keep your voice from
weeping and your eyes from tears, for the reward
for your work will come–this is the LORD's declaration–
and your children will return from the enemy's land.
Jeremiah 31:16

The Lord proclaimed through His faithful prophet, Jeremiah, that trouble would be coming one day soon for His people. Their years of rebellion against Him would bring about destruction in the land. For too long they had ignored His ways and devoted themselves to pagan idols. The time would come when their land would fall into Babylonian hands. In the faraway land, they would grieve the loss of everything the Lord had given them in Israel. But there was good news. The Lord wouldn't keep them exiled in Babylon forever. He assured His people that one day He would allow them to return to Israel and worship Him with a pure heart. For that reason, He encouraged them to stop crying and start looking for a new day of hope that would dawn in His time.

When we are in painful situations, it is easy to get stuck in our tears and forget that through Christ we always have hope in the future. People often say that tears drain the pain of our grief. Crying is important, but despite the difficulty of our circumstances, the Lord intends for us to turn from weeping to living in hope that centers in Him.

Father, I am grateful for the way You enable me to turn my weeping to trusting. Lord, dry my tears, and help me to remember that everything You do is for my good. Help me to follow Your guidance, no matter what the consequences.

A Legacy of Fear

Do this so that you may fear the LORD your God
all the days of your life by keeping all His statutes
and commands I am giving you, your son, and your
grandson, and so that you may have a long life.
Deuteronomy 6:2

When we are young, we do not always think about the legacy that we have received. However, as we grow older, we become more concerned about the legacies we will pass on to the next generation. We begin to give more of our attention to the virtues we will instill in the people we love. The Lord spoke through Moses to command His people about the legacy He intended for them to give to their children and grandchildren. He wanted them to leave a legacy of fearing the Lord. A legacy of fear does not imply that we teach our children to be terrorized by the Lord's presence. Quite the opposite, it means we show them how to have intimate fellowship with the Lord. Fearing Him means nurturing a healthy respect for Him that blends our love for Him with our eagerness to take Him seriously. Fearing the Lord is recognizing His ultimate power and authority over all things, but trusting that He would never use that power against us. When we show the people who look up to us how to fear the Lord, we give them a priceless legacy that will last forever.

Father, strengthen me to leave a legacy of fearing You. Allow me to be a witness for You to my family and friends. Let my love for You shine so brightly that no one questions where my loyalty lies.

Fight the Good Fight

Fight the good fight for the faith; take hold of eternal
life that you were called to and have made a good
confession about in the presence of many witnesses.
1 Timothy 6:12

What would you consider to be a good fight? Some people think a professional boxing match with lots of entertaining twists and turns is a good fight. Others have the opinion that a fight is good if it ends with a surprising knockout punch. These perspectives are valid, but a Christian's fighting "the good fight for the faith" has nothing to do with entertainment. Timothy served in a setting in which some believers had become distracted. Avoiding the temptation to be just as distracted would put Timothy in the throes of a spiritual fight. In the clash, an eagerness to walk in the path of selfish desires would be set against a steady walk of sincere faith in and obedience to Christ. "The good fight" would require that Timothy defend the truth and choose Christ-like behaviors, attitudes, and habits. Fighting the good fight isn't about making it look good; it's about fighting the fight worth fighting. Keeping your life in obedience to Christ is worth fighting for! Every day, growing believers faithfully step up and fight against the temptation to be distracted from our commitment to the Lord. This is not a one-time fight, it is lifelong! Get up every morning ready to fight the good fight, and stay faithful to the Lord.

Father, show me how to take on the good fight of faith for Your glory. Give me strength today, and every day to stay faithful to You in everything that I do.

Father's Last Instruction

"Keep your obligation to the LORD your God to walk
in His ways and to keep His statutes, commands,
ordinances, and decrees. This is written in the
law of Moses, so that you will have success in
everything you do and wherever you turn."
1 Kings 2:3

While we should always think before we speak, there are certain conversations where we put more thought into our words. The last instructions to the babysitter before you leave for a long night. The last conversation before a loved one moves away. The last conversation with someone before they pass away. We recognize the importance of last words and using the final moments to remind a person of what is most important.

King David left Solomon, his son, a compelling instruction before he died. He instructed Solomon to walk with God. David wanted to make sure that even if he forgot everything else, this Solomon would remember. In due time, Solomon learned to treasure his father's instruction, but this instruction is not just for Solomon. David's instruction echoes across the centuries to us. We are wise if we heed what he said, and we are sure to agree that he instructed us well. Are you keeping your obligation to the Lord? What instructions are you choosing to ignore? What would your last instructions be?

Father, today I commit to putting the instruction from Your Word to work in my life. Lord, help me to stay focused on Your will, and not to be distracted by the things of this world. Remind me daily of David's words to Solomon, and let them guide me to keep Your Word.

The Down Payment

He is the down payment of our inheritance,
for the redemption of the possession,
to the praise of His glory.
Ephesians 1:14

When making a large purchase, such as a home, a down payment is often required to guarantee the intent to purchase. This can be quite a large sum, depending on the size of the purchase. Once the purchase agreement is finalized, the purchaser can begin to enjoy the many benefits of ownership. If you have purchased a home, perhaps you recall the feelings of joy and satisfaction but also the feeling of responsibility and commitment. You would not put a large sum of money down easily or without the full intention of following through. The indwelling of the Holy Spirit is the guarantee of the redemption of the believer purchased by Jesus Christ on the cross. The Holy Spirit assures the purchase will be completed when Christ comes to claim His own. At that time, God will bring about final redemption—life in His eternal presence—to all who have received His Spirit.

This spiritual down payment guarantees believers are never in danger of losing their salvation. Thus, believers live with joy and praise for all Christ has done.

They also know the responsibility and commitment that come with being children of God in Christ.

Father, my heart overflows with gratitude for salvation through Jesus, the security of the Holy Spirit, and the promise of eternity in heaven. Thank You for giving me the Holy Spirit to guide me, teach me, and give me assurance of my eternal salvation.

Reason to Hope

Even if He causes suffering, He will show compassion
according to His abundant, faithful love.
Lamentations 3:32

In spite of repeated warnings and calls to repentance, God's people continued to disobey His Word and expectations. His mercy and patience were not to be taken for granted, and His people were not to assume they would not suffer the consequences of sin. Jerusalem was besieged, the walls breached, and the temple destroyed by 586 BC. Although God takes no delight in the suffering of His people, He does permit the consequences of sinful choices to take effect. The book of Lamentations shows the crying out of the people of God. Even during dark and difficult times, even after the people of Israel had failed again and again, God remained merciful, and His compassion far outweighed the sorrow.

Have you ever gotten to the point where you feel overwhelmed with suffering? Maybe you're in that place now. Even though the Lord allows consequences for sin, He does not reject His people forever. He uses setbacks, loss, and affliction to accomplish His sovereign purposes. He disciplines His people with the goal of restoring them into a right fellowship with Him. Thus, we learn from Him and have hope in Him who is filled with compassion and abundant in mercy toward all who believe. No matter where you are, what you are suffering, or what consequences you are paying, God has compassion for you, and desires you to have your hope in Him.

Lord, may my faith remain strong, regardless of my circumstances, because my hope is in You. Help me to remember to praise You even in the depths of my despair.

Calling All Sinners

Go and learn what this means: I desire
mercy and not sacrifice. For I didn't come
to call the righteous, but sinners.
Matthew 9:13

Christians live in a world that does not always appreciate our sense of what is right, our faith convictions, and our commitment to a godly lifestyle. Nevertheless, we must guard against developing an attitude where we think we are better than those who do not believe or act as we do. Blinded by their own sense of piety and arrogance, the Pharisees thought they were the only ones in right standing with God. Hence, they were openly critical of Jesus for eating and interacting with people who did not keep the ritual sacrifices as they did. Jesus responded by calling their attention to the words of the prophet Hosea (6:6). God is more interested in a person's loyal love than He is the ritual of sacrifice. Sacrifices are worthless when given to the Lord without mercy toward others. Jesus came to save humble sinners, not the self-righteous who fail to see their need for Him. Like Jesus, we are to reach out to sinners so that they may know Jesus' grace, love, and mercy. It is not an easy task to show grace while still speaking truth, but this is the balance that we as Christians have been called to. This is what it means to truly love people.

Father, give me courage to step out of my comfort zone to share the gospel with others. Help me to love people the way You love! It is only with Your strength that I will be able to share the truth of the gospel and give grace. Remind me of this balance, and give me the love to pour out to everyone I encounter.

Liberty for All

You are to consecrate the fiftieth year and proclaim
freedom in the land for all its inhabitants. It will
be your Jubilee, when each of you is to return
to his property and each of you to his clan.
Leviticus 25:10

Have you ever felt trapped by your circumstances? They may even be ones that you know are your own fault, but you don't know how to get out. The desire and need to be set free is universal and timeless. Individuals, groups, even entire nations yearn for liberty. Perhaps, no greater bond exists than among a people who want freedom from oppression. For Israel the fiftieth or jubilee year was to be treated as holy unto the Lord. It was a time of great celebration for all of Israel. Debts were cancelled, land reverted to its original owners, and those who had sold themselves into slavery were set free. As a result, burdens were eased, dignity was restored, and families were reunited. The slate was wiped clean. As Americans, we celebrate our liberty as a nation. As believers in Christ, we know another level of liberty. All people are bound by the chains of sin. Jesus came to this earth to bring release and liberty to all! If you have accepted Jesus as Your Lord and Savior, then you are free! Thus, we proclaim liberty in Christ throughout all the land!

Father, thank You for releasing me from the chains of sin. Thank You for giving me true and absolute freedom! Help me to remember when I feel trapped by my circumstances that I have liberty in You!

For God's Glory

Whenever the spirit from God troubled Saul, David would pick up his lyre and play, and Saul would then be relieved, feel better, and the evil spirit would leave him.
1 Samuel 16:23

Every two years we get the joy of watching people from all over the world come together to compete in the Olympic games. What a joy to watch these talented athletes in their performances on a worldwide stage. Athletes commit themselves to their discipline, and practice thousands of hours until they are skilled, proven, and confident. Often a number of the athletes will acknowledge their dependence on God and give Him glory in their abilities and victories. David went through a similar preparation process, developing weaponry, military, and leadership skills. This passage reveals the Lord even used David's musical talent to bring blessing. The Lord used each of David's skills in some way to accomplish His purposes and to prepare David to ascend Israel's throne. God has gifted each of us in some way. We do well when we commit these gifts to Him. We may never compete on a world stage, perform for national leaders, or ascend a throne; but we can delight when God is glorified through us.

Father, I dedicate my skills and talents to You. Use me to accomplish Your will and bring You glory. Remind me that no matter what my skills are, they can be used for Your glory. Give me opportunities to glorify You!

The Measure of Love

Therefore I tell you, her many sins have been
forgiven; that's why she loved much. But the
one who is forgiven little, loves little.
Luke 7:47

What contrast exists between the two people in this passage! One was a proper male, a Pharisee. The other was a woman, a sinner, likely a prostitute. The Pharisee wrongly considered himself righteous; the woman knew she was a sinner. The Pharisee was proud; the woman was contrite. The Pharisee failed to provide the most basic courtesies to his invited guest. In spite of what others might have thought, the woman openly displayed devotion to Jesus by anointing His feet. The Pharisee believed he had little to be forgiven for; thus, he failed to show any measure of love in return. The woman knew she had much to be forgiven for; thus, she demonstrated lavish love. This woman's response should be seen as normative. Our love for the Lord is not an attempt to win His favor. It is a response to having been granted the favor of His forgiveness.

It is easy to fall into the trap of believing that our sin is not a big deal, believing that we are "good enough" or that we are a "good person." The truth is that nothing we do is good enough to deserve what Christ has done for us. We are sinners and daily we fail to live up to the perfection of Jesus Christ. This truth should cause us to fall to our knees and weep with gratitude. How much do your actions show your gratitude and love for the forgiveness you have received from the Lord?

Father, may I demonstrate love in a measure appropriate to the forgiveness I have received from You. Point out my sins to me, and remind of me how great Your forgiveness is, so that I may love You more fully.

From Rejection to Victory

My God, my God, why have You forsaken me?
Why are You so far from my deliverance
and from my words of groaning?
Psalm 22:1

Could there be any lonelier feeling than believing you have been abandoned by God? Surely not! In this psalm, David bared his soul as he cried out in agony to God. He felt forsaken. We are not told the details of the situation, but it was a painful time. Whatever the circumstances, David knew that without the Lord he would be devastated. Beginning with verse 22, David's tone shifted from rejection to thanksgiving for victory: "I will proclaim Your name to my brothers; I will praise You in the congregation." Either David's prayer of lament, confession, and petition had been answered, or David so keenly anticipated that it would be, he confidently began to express praise to God. You probably recall that the words of verse 1 were on the lips of Jesus as He hung on the cross. The weight of the sin of the world separated Him from His Father. Because of His death, we who were forsaken in sin can claim eternal victory in Him. Thanks be to God!

Father, draw me close to You when I feel alone; protect me when I feel vulnerable. Give me faith to praise You with confidence, knowing that I'm victorious in You. Remind me that even when I feel alone, You are with me.

Prepare Your Heart to Serve

Now Ezra had determined in his heart to
study the law of the LORD, obey it, and teach
its statutes and ordinances in Israel.
Ezra 7:10

Many worthwhile projects, programs, and organizations begin with a wonderful purpose or mission. Over time, however, some begin to veer off course from their original intent. Unless a course correction is made, the original vision can become so blurred that you're moving in an entirely different direction. Israel had veered far off course from the Lord's original design for His people. Eventually, God's judgment came in the form of exile to Babylon. Subsequently, the Lord used Ezra to lead His people. Ezra prepared himself for service, beginning with an internal, spiritual preparation. He first "prepared his heart." His spiritual preparation took him to the Word of God, not just as a subject to be learned but as truth to be obeyed. Having prepared himself, he was able to lead the people, teaching them the things of God. If they were to discover afresh their purpose as God's people, it would come as they learned and obeyed God's Word for themselves. It is no different for us. If we are going to follow Christ fully with our lives, then we must be prepared to do so. We must spend time in God's Word, and with Him in prayer. We must understand the vision for our lives and be able to hear the Lord's voice clearly, or we will easily be led astray.

Father, help me prepare my heart to serve You by studying and obeying Your Word. Help me to set aside the time I need to spend with You. Don't allow me to get distracted by the things of this world, and hold my gaze ever on You.

Death Defeated

The last enemy to be abolished is death.
1 Corinthians 15:26

Death is a stark, and sometimes dark, reminder that we live in a fallen world. Most of us have faced the reality of death through the loss of a loved one or dear friend. Eventually, we will face it ourselves. Death is inevitable. We were born to die. We have made attempts to forestall death. Medical science advancements have resulted in cures for many diseases that in earlier human history led to the death of thousands. We are grateful for these advances, but in the long run, all attempts to avert death will fail. That is, except one. Through Christ's resurrection, all enemies of the Lord have been vanquished, including the greatest enemy of all—death. This is the good news! By His own death, Jesus paid the price to redeem us from death and the grave. By His resurrection, He conquered death and gave us the victory. Yes, physical death still will come to us all (unless the Lord returns first). However, death is not the end for believers in Christ, but rather a transition into the presence of the Lord, where we will live in heaven.

Father, thank You for defeating death and giving eternal life to all who believe. Lord, thank You for removing any reason I could have to fear death. In You alone I have eternal life!

Freedom to Talk to God

Since You, my God, have revealed to Your servant
that You will build him a house, Your servant has
found courage to pray in Your presence.
1 Chronicles 17:25

If you grew up in church, you were probably taught that you could speak directly to God through prayer at a very early age. We are lucky to live in a culture where praying, both in the home and at church, is commonplace. Speaking directly to God is modeled and encouraged. Even with this ease of access, it is difficult to learn to be comfortable in sharing deep longings, brokenness, fears, and desires. Learning to listen for God's voice to reveal His will adds another level. King David felt comfortable opening his heart to the Lord. His boldness was tempered by his humility and reverence. David acknowledged he was the servant and the Lord was God. Everything David had become was a testimony to the faithfulness and blessings of God.

God grants each of us freedom to call upon Him at any time, in any place, in any situation or circumstance. He desires to have a relationship with each of us where we are fully at peace with being open and honest with Him. We can confidently bring all matters, both large and small, to God in prayer. He will hear us and respond to us in ways that bring blessings to our lives and glorify Him.

Father, thank You for the gift of prayer and for the freedom to talk to You anywhere and anytime. Give me the faith to come confidently before You!

A Royal Family

The neighbor women said, "A son has been born
to Naomi," and they named him Obed. He was
the father of Jesse, the father of David.
Ruth 4:17

"It takes a village" is not just a meaningless saying. We were built for community, and in all cultures people come together to take care of one another. The elderly who are no longer able to work rely on the group for their livelihood, and young mothers rely on the wisdom of the elders in raising their children. In the book of Ruth, Naomi had a direct hand in the care of Obed, the son born to Boaz and Ruth. Everyone in the community respected her. Obed grew up and eventually became grandfather of the royal King David, a man after God's own heart. No one knows how much influence Naomi may have had on the family line, but if Ruth's love for Naomi is any indication, she was definitely a big part of their lives. Most American congregations have "church mothers." You know these women. They are the ones that offer to hold every crying baby, teach Sunday school to preschoolers, give wisdom to struggling parents. They offer a wealth of information and assist in a variety of ways. Let's not overlook their contributions. Many of these dear ladies want to give themselves to the work of the church. And one day, children under their influence may have a royal influence themselves.

Father, thank You for the valuable contributions of godly women in our church. Help me to be thankful for their willingness and open hearts.

Love Like Jesus

"I give you a new command: Love one another. Just as I have loved you, you must also love one another."
John 13:34

When Jesus gave this commandment, He had just finished washing His disciples' feet. The Lord of all creation performed a task usually reserved for the lowliest of servants. Those men didn't deserve such tender treatment from Jesus. Within hours, Jesus would be arrested, and His disciples would desert Him. Jesus showed them His love anyway. Jesus was showing them not just how to love one another, but the importance of loving well.

Have you ever shown love to a person, even when you had other things on your mind? Have you ever had someone put you first even when you know how much they have on their plate? This is what it means to love one another. Jesus taught this commandment and demonstrated its meaning by washing dusty, undeserving feet. We, too, are to show love like that.

Dear Father, show me today how I can exhibit real love in a practical way. Open my eyes to the opportunities all around me to show Your love to my friends, family, strangers, and even enemies. Give me the grace to forgive and to put others above myself—and the humility to know that this kind of love is only possible through You.

Being Right vs. Doing Right

For the ways of the LORD are right, and the righteous
walk in them, but the rebellious stumble in them.
Hosea 14:9

The Israelites knew what was right in God's eyes; yet they did not always do what they knew to be right. In fact, they were quick to act according to their passions, desires, and what was expedient for the situation. They seemed to forget, at least for the moment, what God said was right. Rebelliousness does not come as a result of ignorance but of willful disobedience. The Israelites' primary sin was idolatry, which is nothing more than man desiring to control his own actions. After Israel entered the promised land, Joshua commanded them to choose to follow God's way or the ways of idols. The people assured Joshua they would follow God's way. Not long afterwards, the people followed the ways of the pagan gods. Through the prophet Hosea, God again offered His people a choice: choose His way and prosper or choose another way and fail. The prophet's message is true today. God's people are quick to backslide into the ways of the world and are rebellious to God's right way. God offers us a choice with a promise: choose to follow His way and live life to the fullest or follow another way and continually stumble.

Father, thank You for Your precious promise. Help me to always follow Your way, no matter the situation.

Religious Matters

Disregarding the command of God,
you keep the tradition of men.
Mark 7:8

We have all seen the mothers who become horrified if any of her children accidentally lay an item on top of the Bible. In some areas of the South, pastors are not considered appropriately attired if they do not wear a coat and tie in the pulpit. In some churches you could even see a man being kicked out of choir because of the length of his hair. The problem is not in having traditions or personal convictions. My problem is when people develop traditions and then expect others to share the same convictions, even going so far as to judge trespassers as unrighteous. The Pharisees were a very religious Jewish group who prided themselves on their outward religious acts. Not only would they carry out their traditions, but they expected others to follow them as well. They added rules to God's law, thinking that more was better. However, their traditions distracted the people from the true message of God's Word. Traditions become idolatrous when they lead people away from the truth of Scripture. Outward acts never supersede the truth in the heart. It is dangerous to set up unbiblical or added rules for others to follow. Let's look instead to Christ to guide our behavior.

Help me not to place unbiblical burdens on others. Lord, separate out in my heart the convictions that You have given me, and the law You have shown me in the Bible, from the religious traditions that have nothing to do with Your Word. Give me grace in the areas where I fail, that I might be able to give that kind of grace to others.

54

A Few Power-Packed Words

Then He said to them all, "If anyone wants
to come with Me, he must deny himself,
take up his cross daily, and follow Me."
Luke 9:23

Knowing some details of what Jesus went through at His crucifixion, brings a frightening thought to think He might ever call one of us to do the same. The cross reminds us of suffering, pain, rejection, scorn, self-sacrifice, hardship, and even loving and forgiving those who have harmed us. Yet in Luke 9:23, Jesus is calling us to do just that. Jesus wants us as His followers to lay aside our own gain for the sake of others and for His glory. This is not something we could do on our own, but as His followers we have His power and grace to carry us through. As humans, our inclination is to use our own skills, talents, and resources to gratify our own pleasures. Yet, Jesus is calling us to do something radical. He calls you to identify with Him and obey His commands, regardless of the cost. The world teaches you to do just the opposite. Today media pushes us to give our preferences priority. But to follow Jesus, you must do what He did—to serve and not seek to be served. Then you will truly be His disciple.

Father, I need Your grace and power to be able to be a true disciple of Jesus and serve others. Make me more like Jesus everyday.

Matters of the Heart

But the one sown on the good ground–this
is one who hears and understands the word,
who does bear fruit and yields: some 100,
some 60, some 30 times what was sown.
Matthew 13:23

Have you ever seen a passionate gardener tend their plot? During spring they have the tractor and plow ready, and they tear through the soil. Afterward, they fertilize and plant the seeds, carefully covering each one up. Then all rejoice when the first shoots start popping through the soil.

This is the image that Christ gives us. What a wonderful picture He uses to represent the planting of the Word of God into the heart of man. The Holy Spirit prepares the land. The Word germinates and begins to grow and burst forth, creating a new being in Christ. The new believer goes on to produce excellent fruit that continues the cycle of reproduction in the kingdom of God. Man's heart is key. An unrepentant heart will not receive the seed. Only a heart made righteous can produce the fruit of righteousness. We need to repent of all our transgressions so Jesus can use us to further His kingdom and bring God glory.

Father, make my heart one that readily receives Your Word that I may produce much fruit in the world to further Your kingdom. Help me to be a passionate gardener, planting Your Word in the heart of others.

The Great Physician's Surgery

Search me, God, and know my heart; test me and
know my concerns. See if there is any offensive
way in me; lead me in the everlasting way.
Psalm 139:23-24

Psalm 139:23 is an open invitation for the Great Physician to come and do surgery on our hearts. Sometimes we have buried sins deep within us, and this sin needs to be revealed by God. They are buried deep, like a cancerous tumor imbedded in our souls. When God searches and reveals them, our response is key to our living righteously and in fellowship with God. The psalmist asked God to destroy his enemies. David equated his enemies with God's enemies because David was "a man loyal to Me" (Acts 13:22). Before David could ask God to judge them, he knew he must ask God to search him out and reveal any sin in his own life. David wanted first to make sure he was right with God before asking for help against his enemies. Once we invite God to examine our hearts, He is faithful to reveal what is there. When our sins are revealed, confession and repentance are the cure. God is faithful. He will make us whole again, no matter how far we have buried our sins within us.

Father, my heart is open to You. Go deep, and reveal sin and disobedience that keeps me from being right with You. I know it will be a painful healing process, but I also know it is far worse to let the cancer rampage.

What Kind of Water Are You Drinking?

"In fact, the water I will give him will become a well
of water springing up within him for eternal life."
John 4:14

When God created men and women, He placed a yearning in their hearts to worship Him. He created humanity for fellowship and to be glorified. However, sin entered humanity and corrupted us from that purpose. We still have that yearning within us to worship someone or something. We strive to satisfy this yearning, best illustrated by the thirsty soul seeking to be quenched. The woman at the well was interested in what Jesus offered, perhaps first thinking Jesus was offering her an inexhaustible supply of fresh water. She would never have to carry water again! But Jesus spoke of what quenches the spiritual thirst in a person, a need that goes far deeper than the physical desire. Only what Jesus offers can fully quench what we long for spiritually. The Living Word, Jesus Christ, comes abundantly and with inexhaustible supply. All we have to do is open up our hearts, repent, and let Him fill us by faith with His love and forgiveness. Only Jesus can quench the thirsty soul.

Father, thank You for giving me what I most need—Living Water that's always free and quenches my thirsty soul.

Facing Life's Fears

Immediately Jesus spoke to them.
"Have courage! It is I. Don't be afraid."
Matthew 14:27

Jesus came to bring us peace. In fact, He is called the Prince of peace. The wrath and judgment of God against sin may promote fear in the heart to draw us to Him. But the end result is that we can have peace with God and confidence of spending eternity with Him. Many people go through life living in fear. Some are deathly afraid of spiders. Some people even fear butterflies. Many fear falling or flying, and some fear the future. But with Jesus, we do not have to live with the fear of death and judgment. The disciples saw what they thought was an apparition coming toward them in the night, walking on top of the water. Who can blame them for their fear? Yet it was Jesus, and He spoke to them to calm their fear. The message is clear: When Jesus is with us, we can be confident in any situation; we have no reason to be afraid. He will see us through any predicament or malady because we have His promise that He will never leave us. Our future is secure in Christ, and even death has no power over us. He is the Prince of peace.

Father, with Jesus my fears fade away. You are with me always, even to the end of the age. Thank You that with You I can get through anything this life throws at me.

Believe and Be Blessed

Jesus said, "Because you have seen Me,
you have believed. Those who believe
without seeing are blessed."
John 20:29

Missouri is the "Show Me" state, implying that Missourians are skeptical until physically shown that something is true or real. Many people have the same view. They take what people tell them with a grain of salt and wait to see the evidence. We live in a culture of skeptics and critics. Perhaps we have been fooled or deceived too many times, or perhaps we have just been taught too many times that people lie. Evidently Thomas had some of that same "show me" tendency. Since he had been absent when Jesus first appeared, Thomas would not believe simply based on the word of others. He wanted to physically see for himself that Jesus was alive. When the Lord appeared a second time, and Thomas saw Him, he exclaimed, "My Lord and my God!" (v. 28).

We haven't seen the physically resurrected Christ, but we've heard from eyewitnesses through the pages of the Bible. We have experienced the truth that dwells in our hearts. Our lives have been radically changed, as have the lives of so many others. A physical appearance would not make Jesus any more real than He is right now. The hymn "He Lives" by Alfred H. Ackley says it this way: "You ask me how I know He lives? He lives within my heart!"

Father, thank You for providing proof that Jesus is real and alive through the testimony of Your Word. Help remove the doubts from my heart, and allows me to see the evidence for what it is. Help me have faith through everything I cannot see.

The Ultimate Solution

For Christ also suffered for sins once for all,
the righteous for the unrighteous, that He might
bring you to God, after being put to death in the
fleshly realm but made alive in the spiritual realm.
1 Peter 3:18

Ask people what the greatest problem in the world is, and you will get a myriad of answers: the economy, poverty, hunger, greed, or misused power. But Christians know the main problem in the world is the problem that has plagued humanity since the garden of Eden: sin. It is good to know that in heaven there will be no sin, and, therefore, there will be no problems! Satan is skilled at distracting people from the problem of sin. He keeps people focused on the cares of the world and selfish gain. Until our world recognizes the problem of sin, suffering, pain, fear, and anxiety will continue. Interestingly, there is a solution to the problem that most people ignore. Jesus came to free people from the power of sin and death and to rid the world of its pressing problem. His atonement on the cross solved the problem—if only people would repent and believe in Him. We cannot solve the problem with human power. The only solution is to put our faith in Christ, and He'll make all things right again.

Father, I acknowledge that Jesus is the solution to the greatest problem of the world. Thank You for giving me the opportunity to know Christ and be free from sin's power.

People Need Love and Mercy

"The second is: Love your neighbor as yourself.
There is no other command greater than these."
Mark 12:31

Loving God is easy. Think of all God has done for you: protected you from enemies; given you a loving family; provided you with shelter, food, and clothing; and most of all, died for you so your sins could be forgiven, and you could live with Him for eternity. It's easy to love someone who has done all this. But Jesus commands us to love our neighbor, and that is much harder! God desires to have fellowship with people. He made people to be like Him and to have fellowship with one another. But some people make it very difficult! In His mercy God has set you free and released you from a debt you could not pay. If you are truly grateful for all He has done, then you must pass on His mercy and love to others. Without God's mercy and love, people will be destined for everlasting darkness. Without second thought we are called to show mercy and love to our enemies as well as our friends. The greatest gift you can give them is to show them the love and forgiveness of Christ.

Father, I am nothing without You. I love You with all my heart. Help me to also love my neighbors as myself. They are lost without You.

Behave Wisely

I will pay attention to the way of integrity.
When will You come to me? I will live with
a heart of integrity in my house.
Psalm 101:2

Parents often say to their children: "We're going out to dinner tonight. Be on your best behavior." But "your best behavior" may not necessarily be wise behavior. The beginning of wisdom is to know and fear the Lord. And wise behavior—knowing and fearing God—should begin at home and extend to all other places and activities. When King David said, "I will live with a heart of integrity in my house," he knew that such power of behavior came only from God. Yet, knowing this, David still let his personal desires and inconsistent discipline with his children cause him to make bad decisions without seeking God's wisdom. As a result, his home life suffered tragic consequences, reflected in both his public and private spiritual life. Our culture today screams: "Look out for number one! Do what feels good! Have no moral absolutes!" Many Christians are being seduced into this philosophy, not seeking God's wisdom. As a result, families disintegrate and society suffers. Only with God's presence and power in our daily lives can we "pay attention to the way of integrity."

Father, give me wisdom in my home life and enable me to reflect it in my public behavior as well. Give me the strength to be able to do what is wise, rather than what is easy.

Endure Hardship

But as for you, be serious about everything,
endure hardship, do the work of an
evangelist, fulfill your ministry.
2 Timothy 4:5

Paul's second letter to Timothy was an encouraging reminder of Timothy's spiritual heritage and personal faith. But Paul also warned Timothy of perilous times and perilous people who would creep into the church, having a form of godliness, but denying the power of God. Paul concludes this warning with a charge: Preach the Word! To those who don't want to hear sound doctrine, whose ears itch to hear only what pleases them, who turn from truth to worldly philosophy: Preach the Word! This charge, along with its subsequent challenge to endure afflictions, is especially relevant to anyone who carries a role in church leadership. When the Word is preached or taught in its entirety, a believer runs the risk of being labeled legalistic, intolerant, or even out of touch with reality. Preaching the Word may offend. Attendance could be impacted, and offerings might temporarily decline. But the charge in God's Word is clear: Teach the Word and endure the subsequent hardship. Spread the gospel and fulfill your ministry for the cause of Christ. Never forget what Christ endured for you.

Father, give me courage to teach Your Word and to endure hardships. Remind me of the importance of sharing Your Word and how small my fears are in comparison.

Manifest God's Works

"Neither this man nor his parents sinned,"
Jesus answered. "This came about so that
God's works might be displayed in him."
John 9:3

Jesus sometimes did unorthodox things in order to show God's power at work. For example, one day He spat on the ground, made clay with His spit, rubbed the clay on a blind beggar's eyes, and told him to wash it off in a nearby pool. When the beggar obeyed and washed off the clay, he came back seeing! It's amazing how God works: be obedient to Christ and God will manifest Himself in magnificent ways.

It is like a child that is doing poorly in school. The teacher keeps telling them to study, but the student doesn't listen and keeps failing. When they are young they do not understand that the teacher is trying to help them. Finally, the student decides to study and succeeds! That's how God works. He gives us all the answers; He shows the path to follow. All we have to do is be obedient and follow Christ's example and God will manifest Himself.

Father, may I see Your manifestation daily as I am obedient to Christ. Help me to remember that even if I do not understand what You are asking me to do, it is not my part to understand Your ways, it is my part to obey and follow You.

Finding God's Purpose

I chose you before I formed you in the womb;
I set you apart before you were born. I
appointed you a prophet to the nations.
Jeremiah 1:5

Jeremiah warned the people of Judah that their continued disobedience to God would lead to their downfall. They scorned him and continued living unrepentant lives. But Jeremiah kept preaching—for forty years. And then Judah fell. Surely Jeremiah wanted to scream, "No more! I quit!" But I imagine he remembered that life-changing day when God said to him, "Before I formed you, I knew you and called you to be my prophet. I'll be with you, so don't be afraid." From that moment, Jeremiah knew God's purpose for his life; that is what kept him going. When you are sure of your calling, it is easy to not lose hope, because even in the hard times, you can know that you are succeeding just by the fact that you are following where God has called you. Find your God-given spiritual gifts through Bible study, prayer, and wise Christian counsel. Discover God's call and purpose for your life.

Father, empower me to fulfill Your purpose in my life. Help me to find the faith that I need to plow fully into the task You have set before me.

The Right Focus

Therefore, any one of you who judges is without excuse. For when you judge another, you condemn yourself, since you, the judge, do the same things.
Romans 2:1

It's all about focus. You've probably heard the old saying, "Every time you point a finger in judgment at someone else, you have three fingers pointing back at yourself." Paul goes even further and says it's inexcusable to judge anyone because we all sin. Perhaps your sins are different from another person's, but sin is sin. (Review the sin list Paul sets out in Romans 1.) So we have the mistaken notion that if we focus on someone else's sins, we don't have to deal with our own, which is inexcusable. Therefore, the next time we want to make a judgmental remark, we'd be wise to realize while that may not be a sin we struggle with, we all struggle with sin in various forms. Get the focus back on personal sins and forgiveness. In judging, we may unintentionally focus on condemnation and not on God's goodness, which leads to repentance. Conversely, if we focus on God's goodness and grace, and on the need to remove the sin in our own lives, we will be less likely to put others down for their sins, and more likely to repent of our own shortcomings. It's all about focus.

Father, may my focus be on Your goodness and grace and not on judging others. Help me to remember that no one's sin is better or worse than my own, and that we are all equally in need of forgiveness.

A Perspective on Contentment

Your life should be free from the love of money.
Be satisfied with what you have, for He Himself
has said, I will never leave you or forsake you.
Hebrews 13:5

Despite his beatings, harassment, shipwrecks, and alienation from his fellow Jews, Paul still did his best to spread the gospel of Jesus Christ. And while in prison, he wrote to the Philippians saying that no matter what his circumstances were, he had learned to be content. Contentment has to do with attitude—not circumstances. Contentment transcends circumstances and brings an inner sense of peace, even when we are sad, lonely, grieving, and financially challenged. It does not remove emotions or mean that we cannot feel sadness or anger; but it means even through those feelings we have absolute faith. Outwardly, we may suffer, but internally, we can rest assured that the Christ who saved us has also fulfilled His promise to send His Holy Spirit to live within us, to empower us, and to comfort us. He will never leave us or forsake us. Believing this promise should spur us on to do the best we can with what we have, where we are, for Jesus' sake today. That's contentment.

Father, may I be content but not complacent. Help me rely on You, whatever my circumstances. Help me find contentment not in the things of this world, or in my present circumstances, but in You.

Alone Time with God

I am at rest in God alone;
my salvation comes from Him.
Psalm 62:1

Often faith puts us on the move, but sometimes faith keeps us waiting for God to move. Waiting is usually difficult for us. Yet over and over again, Scripture admonishes us to be still, to wait on the Lord. As he waits, the psalmist acknowledges first of all that salvation comes from God. His enemies may be powerful, but God is all-powerful; knowing that gives him the strength to wait on God. God is never late, but He's also never in a hurry. He acts in His time, not ours. So when we are in God's waiting room, it's a good time for us to be alone with Him, not to fret, but to get to know Him better. One way to know Him better is to meditate on His Word. For example, pay close attention to the statement David repeats twice in the verses surrounding this verse. These words are powerful: "He alone is my rock and my salvation, my stronghold; I will never (not) be shaken" (vv. 2, 6). If we meditate on these words and receive them into our waiting souls, not only will we not be moved, we'll not even be shaken.

Father, thank You for being my rock. And most of all, thank You for the gift of my salvation. Keep me strong in my waiting, and help me to have the patience to understand the importance of Your timing. Give me guidance on how to use my time of waiting, and allow it to be a time where I can move closer to You.

United with Christ

"I am the vine; you are the branches. The one
who remains in Me and I in him produces much
fruit, because you can do nothing without Me."
John 15:5

In order to make His disciples clearly understand the necessity of maintaining a close relationship with Him, Jesus used the allegory of the vine. The disciples were aware that the vine had become the symbol for the nation of Israel. When Jesus said, "I am the vine," He was agreeing with Isaiah and Jeremiah, who portrayed Israel as a wild and degenerate vine. But Jesus was the true vine. The purpose of a vine is to have branches that bear fruit—not just a few little grapes, but large clusters of delicious, mouth-watering fruit that make the taste buds tingle. For this to happen there must be a continuous flow of nourishment from the vine into the branches. If the branches are cut off from the vine, they can no longer grow; they will dry out and die. The same is true if we want to be productive branches of Christ. We must be attached to and constantly fed by Him. This happens through our obedience, because when we obey, our spiritual blood vessels unclog, and we receive His life-giving nourishment. Without Him, the Bible says we can do nothing.

Father, by abiding in You through obedience, may I indeed produce much fruit. Help me to stay faithfully attached so that I may continue to grow in You.

How the World Was Won

The peacemakers are blessed, for
they will be called sons of God.
Matthew 5:9

It's no wonder the religious leaders of Jesus' day hated Him and His seemingly strange and radical ideas. One of His most thought-provoking statements was recorded in Matthew 5:9. Peacemakers? Really? Israel was looking for a conquering king who would deliver them from Roman oppression. For them a peacemaker meant a warrior. It meant someone who would bring peace by destroying the opposition. But Jesus wasn't speaking of a warring peacemaker—at least not in the physical sense. Today, if the officials of two warring countries negotiated a peace agreement, they would be considered peacemakers. Is this what Jesus was talking about? No, because world peace is short-lived, and the peace of which Jesus spoke lasts forever. It's the peace that passes all understanding, the peace that only He can give. He told His disciples that in the world they would have tribulation, but to cheer up for He had overcome the world. He was leaving them His peace, which they were to spread by telling others how to have peace with God through salvation in Him alone. We who have His peace are to do the same. Tell others. Be peacemakers. Win the world to Christ.

Father, as I pray for world peace, may I most of all be diligent in telling others how to have peace with You. Lord, I know that true peace can only be found in You. Help me to remember to see You for who You truly are, and not for what I imagine You should be.

Godly Compassion

Now Jesus summoned His disciples and said,
"I have compassion on the crowd, because they've
already stayed with Me three days and have nothing
to eat. I don't want to send them away hungry;
otherwise they might collapse on the way."
Matthew 15:32

Jesus healed the sick, gave sight to the blind, and made the lame walk. The people were amazed and gave glory to God. Jesus also took the opportunity to gather His disciples and teach them a few lessons. First, He taught them to see the crowds through His eyes. Even though they were not asking for food, Jesus was aware of their hunger and had an overwhelming desire to give them something to eat. He didn't just empathize with their situation; Jesus took action. Sometimes we get so caught up in doing the Lord's work that we miss even the most basic needs of those around us. Compassion is not merely observing the needs of others; it's always accompanied by a desire to ease their suffering. Jesus also taught the disciples to rely on the power and provision of God when it seems you have nothing to give. Another miracle! They fed 4,000 people with fish to spare. Developing godly compassion is important and takes daily practice.

Father, open my eyes to those around me who are in need of both physical and spiritual sustenance. Give me opportunities to meet the needs of the people around me, and the strength to follow through. Help me to give sacrificially, knowing that in the end, You will provide what I need.

All Are Welcome

But in every nation the person who fears Him
and does righteousness is acceptable to Him.
Acts 10:35

Historically it was against religious protocol for Jews to associate with Gentiles. In the previous verses of Acts 10, the Holy Spirit revealed to Peter that no person, regardless of race or ethnicity, should be considered common or unclean. He was then sent to the home of Cornelius, a Gentile, to tell him about Jesus Christ, His death on the cross, and His resurrection from the dead. Cornelius and his entire household heard the message, believed, and received the Holy Spirit. Then and now, the gospel is for every person on the earth. Jesus' arms were spread wide on the cross to welcome people from every tribe, tongue, and nation into His kingdom.

This was not an easy lesson for the Jesus' Jewish followers to hear. They had learned their entire lives to stay clear of these people, and suddenly they were told to welcome them in? For many of us, sharing the gospel with the nations doesn't even require a passport. God is bringing the nations to our neighborhoods, and he is calling us to serve them. There are no exceptions of, "as long as it's safe", or "as long as they don't scare you", or "as long as they are the same as you." Who is God telling you to welcome?

Father, I want to be used by You to spread the gospel. Open my eyes to divine opportunities to share the gospel with people next door, down the street, and around the world. Remove my fear of the unknown, and help me to love people with Your love.

Wise beyond His Years

"Now grant me wisdom and knowledge so that I may lead these people, for who can judge this great people of Yours?"
2 Chronicles 1:10

Solomon was young and inexperienced when he became king of Israel. Early in his reign, God offered to give Solomon whatever he asked. Solomon asked for wisdom in order to lead God's people. It was an insightful request from such a young man. He knew without help from God that he would be unable to fulfill his duties as king. Pleased with his request, God not only gave him wisdom, but He also lavished him with riches. Solomon became world renowned for both his wisdom and his wealth. Solomon understood that material wealth is meaningless. Wisdom, he said, was worth more than silver or gold—or fancy cars, big houses, or stock portfolios. Later on, Solomon wrote that true happiness comes from fearing God and obeying His commands. No matter our age, we should seek wisdom from God. Wisdom, however, comes with responsibility. God will give us wisdom to discern between right and wrong, but it is up to us to choose the right path, to obey or disobey. Solomon was successful when he walked with God; he failed miserably when he chose his own way.

Father, help me to not only understand what is right but also to do what is right. Help me to seek wisdom in all circumstances and to never choose the easy way out.

Heavenly Focus

Set your minds on what is above,
not on what is on the earth.
Colossians 3:2

Paul, writing from prison, exhorts the believers in Colossae to live with their hearts and minds focused on heaven. This is not our natural inclination. Our natural drift is toward the things of this world. In his Colossians and Philemon MacArthur New Testament Commentary, volume 12, John MacArthur wrote: "The believer's whole disposition should orient itself toward heaven, where Christ is, just as a compass needle orients itself toward the north." Christ is our true north. It takes intentional effort to turn our minds and hearts toward heaven. We are more likely to think about our next project, our next relationship, or our next big thing than we are to think about heaven. Not that we shouldn't concentrate on the here and now. We just have to keep it in the right perspective, making minor (or major) adjustments to stay centered on our true north. Since we have been raised with Christ, we are no longer to be distracted and pulled away by the things of this world. We have a new life with Christ. Once we were raised with Christ, we became intimately bound with Him. The next time you feel the world dragging you down and are disoriented, look up!

Father, don't let distractions of this world bring me down. Help me to keep my eyes on Jesus who restores my soul. Reorder my priorities so that You are so high above everything else that I am not tempted to shift anything above You.

I Give You My Word

In the beginning was the Word, and the Word
was with God, and the Word was God.
John 1:1

John began his Gospel with a concise and powerful statement about Jesus. "The Word" is a wonderful, descriptive title for Jesus, the Son of God. Jesus is the eternal, preexisting Word-become-flesh. He is the direct message from the Father who reveals His purpose through the very life of Christ. The Word (Jesus) is the Author and Creator of all things. Not one thing was made apart from Him. He was there when the Father spoke the heavens and the earth into being. He was there in the garden when God called out to Adam. He was there when God gave the law to Moses and dwelled among His people in the tabernacle. He was with God and He was God. And now here Jesus is, the culmination of the Father's plan for salvation. The One who made everything, from the highest angel to the lowliest ant, is now here to be our salvation—the Author and Finisher of our faith. Who else is more qualified to offer new life than the One who created life? God gave us His Word, and this is good.

Father, thank You for sending Your Son Jesus into the world to save me. Help me to be a light to others that they might come to know the Light of the world. Give me guidance on how I can share the Word with others.

Itemized Confession

If we confess our sins, He is faithful and righteous to forgive us our sins and to cleanse us from all unrighteousness.
1 John 1:9

Every spring, tax season is upon us. Time to gather our forms and receipts, and document our assets and liabilities. Every digit counts when the accountant begins claiming, deducting, and itemizing. Taxpayers shudder at the thought of an audit. Wouldn't we be surprised if we received a letter stating we had been flagged to be audited spiritually? We'd scramble around gathering old prayer journals, baptism certificates, and giving records. Of course, the idea of a spiritual audit isn't real, but it should cause us to think! God's Word tells us there is an audit of sorts, performed by the Holy Spirit. If we claim to live in the light, the proof is in our staying away from darkness, experiencing fellowship with God and each other, and being cleansed from sin by the blood of Jesus. By claiming we have no sin, we essentially call God a liar. Is the Holy Spirit knocking at your heart's door? Is it time for an audit? Own up to your sins, confess them, receive forgiveness, and let God cleanse you "from all unrighteousness."

Father, help me confess quickly so my sins don't stack up and I can stay in sweet fellowship with You. Help me to remember that while I am saved by faith alone, the fruit in my life is the evidence that I have been saved.

Freedom in Christ

Because the Spirit's law of life in Christ Jesus has
set you free from the law of sin and of death.
Romans 8:2

Have you ever had the opportunity to visit a prison? These people are condemned for breaking man's law. They have been found guilty. Some will only have to serve a few years, but some of them face life sentences. Those who have accepted Christ may be physically in chains, but that is all that is constrained. Through the blood of Jesus, God, in His mercy, has set their spirits free. He has unshackled their souls. Yes, they have painful memories, remorse, and consequences, but they are no longer condemned. Out in the real world, they never experienced the kind of freedom they know now in Christ Jesus. These prisoners are forgiven. Romans 8:2 highlights the freedom that life in Christ offers. Because of His forgiveness, real freedom is available to anyone who asks. Find comfort in the fact that no sin is too big for God to forgive. The law dictated by God to Moses still does its job of pointing out our sin, but regardless of where our sin has left us, in Christ we can be set free. Apart from Him, we will never know true freedom. Have you made the decision to surrender your life to Jesus? New life in the Spirit awaits you!

Father, I believe Jesus, Your Son, died to pay the price for my sin. Forgive me. I commit my life to You. I know that my soul has been wrapped in the chains of sin, and it is only through You that I can have true and absolute freedom.

Designer Creation

The earth and everything in it, the world
and its inhabitants, belong to the LORD.
Psalm 24:1

What a wonderful world God designed for us to live in! From the mountains to the ocean, from the smooth skin and innocence of a newborn baby boy to the elderly woman weathered and worn by the years, beauty is ours to behold. All around us God's creation shines, pointing us to the One who made us. When he penned Psalm 24, David, the man after God's own heart, understood the bigger picture. He knew the Lord does not look on the outward appearance to judge beauty. The Lord looks on our hearts for therein resides the true treasure, a soul surrendered to Christ. When the Holy Spirit works His transforming power, all things are made new. The body bearing a Spirit-filled soul is most beautiful when it shines forth the Savior in both word and deed. What joy to have all of God's earth at our disposal! What joy to be the only one of His creatures capable of knowing His salvation! What joy to belong to God! In what way will you point someone to the Creator today? Go forth and shine!

Father, thank You for the beauty of creation and the beauty of knowing You, my Creator. Help me to keep my eyes open to the beauty that is all around me and not get distracted by what sin has caused in this world. Hold me in awe of You!

Beautiful Feet

And how can they preach unless they are sent?
As it is written: How beautiful are the feet of
those who announce the gospel of good things!
Romans 10:15

Who brought the message of Christ to you? Perhaps it was a parent, teacher, pastor, or friend. Typically we don't think about feet as being particularly beautiful. But consider the journey involved as one believer willingly and lovingly presents the good news to another person. The person did not just wake up one day and decide that they were going to change your life. They changed their life by sharing with you what they had learned and gathered over a lifetime. They shared with you their walk. It's definitely an act of beauty with life-changing implications. We are all called to be missionaries—people with beautiful feet. Each of us is called to share the journey our feet have been on with others. To whom is the Lord sending you? A neighbor, family member, coworker, or someone in a village on the opposite side of the world? Are you willing to go? Will you surrender your feet to be beautifully used?

Father, here I am. Open my eyes to the people You want me to share my story with. Help me to see people with Your love. Send me!

Sincere Devotion

But I count my life of no value to myself, so that I may finish my course and the ministry I received from the Lord Jesus, to testify to the gospel of God's grace.
Acts 20:24

Saul, the well-known Pharisee and persecutor of Christians, was radically transformed into the apostle Paul—the self-denying, letter-writing missionary who met Jesus on the road to Damascus. Paul was chosen by God to be an instrument for taking the Good News to the Gentiles and to kings, as well as to the people of Israel (see Acts 9). Paul was devoted to his calling even when faced with difficult circumstances and suffering. He endured hardships, knowing there was nothing more important than finishing the work the Lord had given him. In Christ, each of us has been given special tasks to do, which play a part in spreading the gospel. Being sincerely devoted and unwavering in our calling is essential to being fruitful. What is one thing you know the Holy Spirit is prompting you to do? Sometimes stepping out in faith is scary—even if it only involves calling to encourage a friend or giving financially. Just remember, God equips us for what He calls us to do.

Father, I want to be sincerely devoted to You. Help me to stay faithful to what You have called me to. Help me to see the areas where You desire to use me. Use me as Your instrument.

True Nourishment

I am the bread of life.
John 6:48

Do you remember bell-bottoms from the '60s? Did you own a leisure suit in the '70s? What about the big-hair look from the '80s? These fashion faux pas all fall into the same category: What were we thinking? Fashion styles may come and go, but the truth of who Jesus is never changes. Jesus performed a great miracle in John 6 that set the framework for the devotional passage. He fed five thousand people with five loaves of bread and two fish (v. 9–11). The people responded with amazement and tried to crown Jesus as king (v. 15). They wanted what Jesus could do for them, but His goal was not personal popularity. Jesus offered salvation for those who were hungry spiritually. Jesus promised everlasting life to those who believed in Him. He was (and is) the Bread of life. (This is one of seven "I am" sayings of Jesus in John.) Jesus contrasted Himself with the manna in the wilderness provided during the time after the exodus (v. 49–51). While the manna came only for a day and was gone by evening, the Living Bread came from heaven and provided eternal life. That Bread never goes out of style.

Father, help me to desire You, not merely the things that You provide for me. Help me to recognize the difference between the things that fade away, and the things from You that are eternal.

Little Guys, Big God

Now faith is the reality of what is hoped
for, the proof of what is not seen.
Hebrews 11:1

Every Hall of Fame is made up of ordinary people who do extraordinary things. In the Country Music Hall of Fame, you find people like Loretta Lynn, the coal miner's daughter, who started life as an ordinary person but achieved stardom through her music. In the Hall of Fame in Cooperstown, you discover Hank Aaron came from humble beginnings in Mobile, Alabama, but he achieved stardom by eclipsing the great Babe Ruth's record for the most home runs in a career. Some see Hebrews 11 as a Hall of Fame of faith. Really it is a list of ordinary people—with an all-powerful God. Abel offered a better sacrifice to God than Cain, and God still is using Abel's story to encourage others (v. 4). Enoch walked with God, and God spared him from death (v. 5). The writer commended Noah for building a boat but highlighted God for warning him (v. 7). He noted that Abraham left his homeland but God provided a place even better than the promised land (vv. 8–10). Are you small in stature or in faith? The writer of Hebrews emphasized that no matter how big or small, people need faith to please God, and He will reward those who "diligently seek him" (v. 6). If you are ordinary, you are exactly the person God can use.

Father, cause me to decrease and You to increase. Help me to see my failings not as weaknesses, but as areas that You can use to show Your strength.

Keepers

Carefully observe the commands of
the LORD your God, the decrees and
statutes He has commanded you.
Deuteronomy 6:17

Fishing can be a fun, relaxing thing for people that are good at it, but extremely frustrating for those that are not. Not being an avid fisherman, it is easy to get annoyed when you catch a fish and have to throw it back because it does not meet the regulations provided by the state. Maybe it's too small or too big. We do not want to have to throw back any—we want to take them all! But how many other places in our lives do we try to pick and choose? In Deuteronomy 6, Moses delivered the Shema to the people as one of his most important messages. He reminded them that they were to love the Lord with all of their hearts. Moses encouraged the people not to test the Lord by not diligently keeping His commandments. God desired to prosper them, but only to the degree that they kept all of His commands. They had a big assignment to conquer the promised land, and to achieve it, they needed to remember to observe the things God had delivered to them. Remember: All of the commandments of God are keepers, not merely the ones that we like!

Father, give me such a fear of You that I desire to keep all of Your commands. Give me the strength to stand firm in your laws, and the humility to remember that it is your strength and not my own.

Loving People

It bears all things, believes all things,
hopes all things, endures all things.
1 Corinthians 13:7

Many people refer to 1 Corinthians 13 as the love chapter. Brides and grooms use it in their wedding ceremonies. Popular Valentine cards use its words for inspiration. However, the passage is about more than romantic love. The love Paul spoke of is God's kind of love, an unconditional love that can endure any circumstance. Loving people love people. Those who have love inside can demonstrate love toward others. If love is not present in you, you can't give it to others. But if you have trusted in Christ and have the love of God in your heart, you can love others even in difficult circumstances. Paul told the Corinthians that love could bear all things. Love caused people to believe even in the most challenging circumstances. Love produces hope and endures many hardships. Love never ends (see 1 Cor. 13:8). Since "God is love" (1 John 4:16), the only way to know love is to know God. When you come to know God, His love is poured into your heart through the Holy Spirit, making you a loving person (see Rom. 5:5). As a loving person, you are able to love people, no matter who they are or what they might have done to you.

Father, fill me with Your kind of love so I can love regardless of circumstances. Help me to love people unconditionally, the way that You have loved me, and do not let my opinions of a person keep me from loving them the right way.

Under the Veil

And the two will become one flesh. So they
are no longer two, but one flesh.
Mark 10:8

Have you ever seen a magician do a trick with ropes? The magician begins by taking two pieces of rope, and after some "magic" words, he makes the two ropes into one. His feat of magic is amazing until you understand the secret behind his "magic." His rope is really one rope but gave the appearance of being two separate pieces.

Marriage is also "a mystery" (Eph. 5:32). God takes two separate individuals (who probably have a lot of loose ends showing) and brings them together as one. But unlike the mystery of the magician, God's mystery is no trick, and is designed to be permanent. From the beginning, God's plan has always been for one man to be married to one woman for all time. Jesus credited God with putting the male and female together (see Mark 10:9), and no man should separate what God brings together. God brings a husband and wife together physically, socially, spiritually, and in every other way. Thank God for the blessings of marriage.

Father, give me a sense of awe about how You take two and make one, sustaining marriage by Your grace. Give me the view of marriage that You have. Remind me that marriage is not an earthly construct, but a covenant relationship that includes You.

What Mercy Means

"Go and learn what this means: I desire
mercy and not sacrifice. For I didn't come
to call the righteous, but sinners."
Matthew 9:13

The Pharisees were powerful religious leaders in the first century
and were Jesus' greatest foes. They placed such an emphasis on
following their interpretation of the law that they showed little
mercy to those who couldn't reach their own unattainable standard.
When Jesus came, however, He spent the majority of His time with
those the Pharisees had disregarded. He forgave a woman caught
in adultery, He healed lepers, and He cast evil spirits from those
who were possessed. In Matthew 9, Jesus sat down and ate with
tax collectors and sinners, which in the eyes of the Pharisees was a
violation of the law of Moses. But Jesus had mercy on those whom
society had shunned. They were spiritually sick, but Jesus knew
He could make them whole. Mercy means that, like Jesus, we will
invest in people who might seem far beyond hope in our own eyes.
Mercy means looking at people through the eyes of Christ and not
evaluating them based on what we see on the surface. Mercy means
seeing everyone as created in the image of God and, therefore,
worthy of our love.

*Father, thank You for sending Your Son to show mercy to me. Help me
relate to others with mercy. Help me to see people with Your eyes, and to
never look at them as beyond Your hope.*

Main Characters

Now finally, all of you should be like-minded
and sympathetic, should love believers,
and be compassionate and humble.
1 Peter 3:8

In a family each person has a role to play. Perhaps you're a grandmother, a mother, or a sister. Maybe you're a grandfather, an uncle, or a nephew. In the first part of chapter 3, Peter spoke specifically to the roles that a wife and a husband play in a marriage. There are character traits unique to the man and unique to the woman. But beginning in verse 8, Peter shared those qualities that everyone as Christians must possess. These are the "main characters." The "main characters" reflect the person of Jesus Christ. Just as He was (and is) sympathetic, loving, compassionate, and humble, we are to be the same. Just as He blessed those who did evil against Him (even to the point of praying for those who sent Him to the cross), we are to do the same. We must strive to be more like Christ in our homes, in our workplaces, and in our communities. There's no greater witness we can have for the gospel than our character and the manner in which we live our lives.

Father, help me to better reflect the perfect character of Your Son so that I may be an effective witness for Your kingdom.

Flighty Promises

As soon as your eyes fly to it, it disappears, for it makes wings for itself and flies like an eagle to the sky.
Proverbs 23:5

We live in a culture obsessed with material things. People work endless hours to make the most money, have the biggest house, and buy the newest car. But when gaining earthly wealth becomes our focus, we invest too much in the temporary and not enough in the eternal. The writer of Proverbs urged his readers not to get caught up in chasing riches, because the wealth of the world is fleeting. When we pass from this earth to spend eternity with the Lord, we won't take one cent we earned with us. This certainly doesn't mean we don't need to work hard in our jobs or whatever task is at hand, but material gain should not be our priority. Jesus gave us clear instructions on what our priority should be in the gospel of Matthew: "But seek first the kingdom of God and His righteousness" (Matt. 6:33). When we keep our eyes set on Him and nothing else—not wealth, success, social status—we can be sure that we're making a worthwhile investment in the kingdom

Father, keep my heart in check when it comes to money and riches. Do not let me be distracted by the earthly definition of success. Keep my eyes on You first and foremost.

Labeled for Life

And when he found him he brought him to
Antioch. For a whole year they met with the
church and taught large numbers. The disciples
were first called Christians at Antioch.
Acts 11:26

Labels can be helpful if they accurately describe the contents of what is inside. At Antioch the followers of Jesus Christ were first labeled as Christians. This happened as a result of the missionary efforts of Barnabas, who first taught the church its purpose and encouraged them to hold tightly to the Lord. Later he found Saul, a former persecutor of the church and brought him to Antioch to disciple him in the ways of Christ. Apparently Barnabas did such a good job in discipling the believers in Antioch that they looked like Christ in the way they lived and related to others. This name was given to the followers of Christ first by those who were outside the faith. They meant it as a term of derision, but the Christians wore it proudly because the label accurately described the contents. Sometimes things and people get mislabeled. The question is not whether you have been labeled, but whether you have been labeled accurately. In today's culture in America, Christian has been a label that people give themselves, and not always accurately. Are you living in such a way that people know you are labeled as Christ's without you saying it?

Father, help me be like Christ in every area of my life. Help Your love to pour out of me so freely that everyone can tell I am a follower of Christ.

Two-Part Trust

Trust in the LORD with all your heart, and do
not rely on your own understanding.
Proverbs 3:5

People have two centers of decision-making in their lives. The first is the head, the seat of reason and logic. When faced with a decision, head-thinkers allow the mind to guide them. Others think from the heart, the seat of emotion and feeling. When faced with a decision, heart-thinkers do what feels right and what creates the least conflict within their emotions. Which thinker is right? The writer of Proverbs suggests those who make decisions should use both the head and the heart—but grounded on trust in the Lord. The writer encourages people to trust in the Lord with their whole hearts. But emotions can deceive and lead to wrong decisions. Likewise, we're encouraged not to rely on our own understanding. The mind can deceive as well. Only the heart and mind guided by trust in the Lord can accurately help in giving direction (Prov. 3:6). The next time you need to make a decision, use your head and your heart. But make sure both of those are guided by trust in the Lord. Allow Him to search your mind and heart for selfishness, fear, or doubt. Listen to Him with both your head and your heart.

Father, guide my head and my heart to trust You more. Remove any lies in me that believe I can do it on my own, or that I have any righteousness without You.

The Difference Is Faith

For in it God's righteousness is revealed
from faith to faith, just as it is written:
The righteous will live by faith.
Romans 1:17

If you've ever recorded your Christian testimony, you probably included a description of your life before Christ in contrast to your life after accepting Him. Perhaps you noted changes in priorities, lifestyle, decision-making, or relationships. One of the most obvious differences, however, is that, unlike unbelievers, Christ followers live by faith—initial faith in Christ for salvation but also daily faith to live a godly life. After all, salvation is from start to finish a work of faith. At the point of salvation, God's righteousness covers us and we are justified by faith to a life of faith. Not only will we live because of our faith, but our faith will determine how well we live. Will we prayerfully seek God's will and His purpose for our lives, our trust in Him growing daily as we know Him better through fervent Bible study and prayer? Will we hear His voice more keenly today because we obeyed Him yesterday? Will we receive more responsibility and blessing tomorrow because we've been faithful in His service today?

Father, I desire to trust You fully. Help my faith to grow as I seek You now in Your Word and prayer.

Christian Intimacy

So if one member suffers, all the members
suffer with it; if one member is honored,
all the members rejoice with it.
1 Corinthians 12:26

Everyone has suffered an injury at some point in their life. Most likely, you have experienced many. When you hurt your hand, it is hard to ignore it and focus on your uninjured parts. When a part is injured, it gets even more attention than it normally has.

Compared to a human body, Paul taught that the church is composed of many members, each indispensable with an important role to fill. When one member suffers or struggles, the other members are to share the pain and restore that one to spiritual health. The focus of the body is on the part that is hurt and in need of help. Just as you would never consider amputation to fix a broken wrist, fellow believers should be so important to us that we strive to keep them vitally connected in our congregations. It is the Lord's desire that we weep with those that are in pain and help them to heal, so that they can fulfill their place in the body of Christ. Equally significant as shared suffering, however, is shared joy, unimpeded by grudges, envy, or rivalry. How it must bless our Lord when His children take such delight in each other! Do you weep with others' suffering? Do you rejoice with their victories?

Father, help us to love each other so sincerely that we weep and rejoice as one body in Christ. Open my eyes to the people in the Church who are hurting, and allow me to hurt with them.

Making the Grade

Mankind, He has told you what is good and what
it is the LORD requires of you: to act justly, to love
faithfulness, and to walk humbly with your God.
Micah 6:8

Did you ever write a paper and receive a low grade because you failed to follow the instructions or answer the assigned question? Maybe you thought that if you wrote enough pages and used enough vocabulary that the teacher wouldn't notice that you never answered the question, and would give you a good grade just for how much effort you put in. In the prophet Micah's day, God's people failed His assignment by substituting religious rituals and empty sacrifices for His requirements of relating to others with justice and mercy, and humbly obeying His will. They thought that if they put in enough effort and did a long enough list of things, that maybe God wouldn't notice that they didn't understand the question. Even today, God's not as interested in our religious activity as He is in our relationship with Him. He's looking for hearts that love Him so unreservedly that they extend His love to others. Do you daily fulfill God's assignment of love? Or are you more interested in making it look like you're putting in the effort, when you really don't understand the question.

Father, I love You. Help me to share Your love and mercy with others. Help me to focus on what is important, and to spend my time the way you desire.

It's Not about the Pastor

I planted, Apollos watered, but God gave the growth.
1 Corinthians 3:6

Every pastor does things a little bit differently, and if you have been in a church long enough, eventually you are bound to hear, "That's not how our former pastor did it." Though the pastor may have served the church many years, the congregation may have had someone who's ministerial dignity and insistence on proper procedure and decorum remain the standard by which some members judge current practices. At the same time, however, other church members praise another former pastor for his approachability, humor, and connection with younger members. Still others hail another pastor's fiery preaching, while some applaud the biblical knowledge of yet another. Paul addressed a similar situation. He agreed that pastors are God's chosen vessels uniquely gifted and sent for a season, but he knew that pastors are only human; they cannot make a church grow in number or a Christian grow in devotion. They can guide, teach, and shepherd the flock God has entrusted to them; but they have to have faith that God will provide the increase, for He's the only One who can.

Father, forgive me when I show greater allegiance to Your servants than to You. Help me to follow the leaders You have placed in my life, and respect them as leaders, but not as saviors. May I remain devoted to Your Son in all my thoughts and deeds.

Gifts from Loving Hearts

Summoning His disciples, He said to them, "I
assure you: This poor widow has put in more
than all those giving to the temple treasury."
Mark 12:43

Have you ever been in a church with people who love to give? I don't mean, just that passes an offering basket; I mean that people's hearts truly desire to give sacrificially? Many churches have a tradition of giving for an annual missions offering. Though joyful expressions are commonplace, tears of humility and gratitude for such an opportunity should be equally typical. How many people give obediently without knowing when they'll receive another paycheck? Are there any who don't know how they'll survive without the funds they just placed in the box? In the passage around the above verse, Jesus pointed out two kinds of givers—those who gave from their abundance and the widow who gave all she had. He did not scold the affluent givers, but He praised the widow. Her sacrifice was impressive and He made her an example for all. Has your giving impressed our Savior, not because of the amount but because of your attitude? Could He use you as an example for others?

Father, thank You for the opportunity to give offerings. May my joyful heart and sacrificial gifts be pleasing to You. Help me to hold everything that You have given me with an open hand, remembering that everything I have belongs to You and is Yours to do with what You will.

Jesus Really Is Counting on Us

But you will receive power when the Holy
Spirit has come on you, and you will be My
witnesses in Jerusalem, in all Judea and
Samaria, and to the ends of the earth.
Acts 1:8

Who hinders unbelievers more from coming to Christ—a believer who verbally witnesses but whose lifestyle fails to support his words, or a believer who lives a godly life but never speaks about Christ? The hypocrisy of one repels listeners from Jesus while the good deeds of another point only to his or her own goodness, but not to the Savior. Jesus said, "You will be My witnesses." He was going away, but His work would continue because His followers would be His witnesses. Today, Jesus' command to witness is equally as compelling for us as it was for the apostles. Wherever we go, with whomever we encounter, Jesus is counting on us to speak and to live out His message. That's His plan for sharing the gospel throughout the earth. What about you? Are you faithfully witnessing both in word and deed? Most of us find it easier to do one over the other, but that is not what God calls us to. Do those you encounter even know you're a Christian? What exactly does your witness tell them about the Savior?

Father, may I daily surrender to the filling of Your Holy Spirit so that I cannot help but share Jesus. Help me to be a witness both in my words and my actions, so that people can see Your love pour out of me, and know that it is from You.

The Most Magnificent of All

Who is He, this King of glory? The LORD of
Hosts, He is the King of glory. Selah
Psalm 24:10

Have you ever been in a country that had a monarch? Or seen on television as a new prince was crowned? It is a unique feeling to be in the presence of royalty. There is a reverence for those with a title, that is not found elsewhere. Although those who are born into the monarchy inherit a royal title and respected status in life, ultimately these people are only human, just as we are. However, as believers, we have the most magnificent of all monarchs. He is Jesus, the King of glory. Though He became human for a time, His righteousness, power, and sovereignty far surpass our experience or comprehension. With title and status both inherited from His Father and earned by His sacrifice, He is due far more than simply our respect; He is worthy of nothing short of pure, unreserved worship.

Father, thank You for Jesus, King of glory. As I come to worship, may I come with a prepared heart, always remembering in Whose presence I stand. Never let me lose my respect and awe when coming into Your presence.

Tenderhearted Forgiveness

And be kind and compassionate to one
another, forgiving one another, just as
God also forgave you in Christ.
Ephesians 4:32

If you have children or have ever been around children, you know that fighting is not something that has to be taught. As soon as a person is old enough to speak, their sinful nature can be easily seen. Parents and teachers go against this by teaching children kindness and compassion. While they did not need to see anyone fight to know how to disagree with someone, they also can see when we do not practice what we preach. How often we teach spiritual truths to children and then forget them ourselves! Paul taught spiritual truths to the believers in Ephesus. Coupled with instructions on kindness, he admonished them to forgive each other. Though vital to Christian well-being, forgiveness is often difficult to practice. It seems easy when we are telling a child to forgive someone for stealing a toy, but how much more difficult it seems when we are the ones needing to forgive. In light of the mercy granted us by Jesus' death on the cross, how dare we arrogantly withhold it from a fellow believer! What an affront to our holy God and His Son's sacrifice.

Father, cleanse all unforgiveness from my heart. May I willingly extend Your forgiveness to others.

Forgave Sins

"But so you may know that the Son of Man has authority on earth to forgive sins," He told the paralytic, . . . "get up, pick up your mat, and go home."
Mark 2:10-11

As Jesus preached in a house in Capernaum, He saw the interceding faith of four friends who went the distance for their paralytic friend. When their way was impeded by the crowds gathered around the house, they tore a hole in the roof and lowered their friend to Jesus. The faith of these four did not reside in their own abilities or in their past accomplishments. Their faith rested in Jesus, the Son of God.

Jesus responded by forgiving the sufferer's sins. Jesus' response shows what human beings need first and foremost. His response addressed the deepest needs of all who were there by displaying His power and authority first in regard to sin, humankind's deepest problem, and then in regard to physical illness. Jesus still has ultimate power and authority over sin and over illness and invites us to come to Him in faith, bringing our friends. When we go to God in prayer, He does not just want us to come for ourselves, but for those we care about, and even for our enemies. He wants us to bring the problems of the world before Him and lay them at His feet.

Father, today I thank You for every act of prayerful intercession ever offered on my behalf. Show me today in whose behalf I ought to act and pray. Show me fellow intercessors with whom I can pray and work. Thank You for forgiving my sins.

Able to Complete

I am sure of this, that He who started
a good work in you will carry it on to
completion until the day of Christ Jesus.
Philippians 1:6

Most young Sunday school students can recount David's courageous stand against Goliath (1 Sam. 17). While watching his father's flock, David had used his slingshot to protect the sheep. He had confidence because he had successfully faced previous challenges. Even more, he had absolute faith that God was with him.

The young shepherd boy took his slingshot, five smooth stones, and the confidence of a man on a mission from God into battle. In the center of God's will, David lost fear; Goliath lost his head. Dwarfed by David's God, Goliath did not have a chance. God, as always, was faithful.

As you look back on your life, can you see God's unseen hand working? If you are God's child, you can rest assured that He will not forsake you and leave His work incomplete. Have you ever felt the complete release of fear when you knew you were in the center of God's will? Only God can give us complete peace in any situation. He is not finished with you yet. You can have confidence that He will continue His work until He is done.

Father, as I reflect on Your work in my life, I thank You for the assurance that You won't quit until You are done. Thank You for Your continuous presence.

A Tax Collector

But Zacchaeus stood there and said to the
Lord, "Look, I'll give half of my possessions to
the poor, Lord! And if I have extorted anything
from anyone, I'll pay back four times as much!"
Luke 19:8

You have guests over for dinner, and about the time you are sitting down to eat, you receive a phone call. The voice on the phone is a monotone, droning on about a bargain that will cost you only $19.99. You wait for the caller to catch a breath so that you can decline the incredible offer.

Tax collectors in New Testament times were regarded with even less sympathy than telephone solicitors receive today. These tax collectors were often dishonest, and frequently they were fellow countrymen who defrauded their friends to collect funds for the Romans and for themselves.

Because of his encounter with Jesus, Zacchaeus' life was turned around. Instead of centering his life on collecting money, he became willing to give it away. After being with Jesus, he proclaimed that he would give half of his possessions to the poor and return fourfold anything he had taken away deceitfully.

Lord, help me to respond to Christ's presence in my life by becoming more like Him. Give me the faithfulness to follow through with my commitments, and with the sacrifices that God has called me to.

More from B&H Books

5 Minutes with God in the Car Line
978-1-4336-4570-9
$9.99

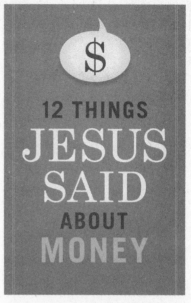

12 Things Jesus Said About Money
978-1-4336-4568-6
$9.99

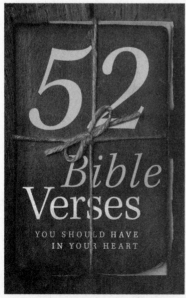

52 Bible Verses You Should
Have in Your Heart
978-1-4336-4569-3
$9.99

30 Days to Your Best Marriage
978-1-4336-4571-6
$9.99